P9-ECN-159

Ex
Libris
JUNE I. SALLAVE

MY ESKIMOS:
A Priest in the Arctic

MY ESKIMOS:

A PRIEST IN THE ARCTIC

ROGER P. BULIARD, O.M.I.

Based on Father Buliard's book **INUK**
and adapted for young readers by Milton Lomask

Illustrated by LEONARD EVERETT FISHER

Vision Books
Farrar, Straus and Cudahy, New York
Burns & Oates, London

VISION BOOKS
IS A DIVISION OF
FARRAR, STRAUS & CUDAHY, INC.

PUBLISHED SIMULTANEOUSLY IN CANADA BY
AMBASSADOR BOOKS, LTD., TORONTO.
MANUFACTURED IN THE U.S.A.

Nihil Obstat:

Rt. Rev. Msgr. Peter B. O'Connor
Censor Librorum

Imprimatur:

✠ Most Reverend Thomas A. Boland, S.T.D.
Archbishop of Newark

The nihil obstat and imprimatur are official declarations that a book or pamphlet is free of doctrinal or moral error. No implication is contained therein that those who have granted the nihil obstat and imprimatur agree with the contents, opinions or statements expressed.

CONTENTS

1. COPPERMINE

"Coppermine! Coppermine!"

Above the chug-chug of the little gasoline cargo schooner, I could hear the Eskimo sailor high in the lookout calling out the name of the port we were approaching.

I was below decks in the smoky engine room. For the last hour, the ship's engineer had been talking to me. He had been describing the wonders—and the horrors—of Eskimoland, that great white section of the world that stretches from Alaska to Greenland, from where the trees stop growing in northern Canada straight up across a score of islands to the North Pole.

My good mother had done her best to teach me manners. Where she had left off, my first instructors, the Christian Brothers of Besançon, France, had taken over. Even so, when I heard the lookout announcing the name of the village I had dreamed of for years, my manners fled. I rushed from the room, leaving the stunned engineer in the middle of a sentence.

On deck, I shoved through passengers and crewmen, squeezing to the rail. It was August, but a snow was falling. It was a slow, wet snow, so thick that, for a moment, I wondered how the lookout could have seen Coppermine. I couldn't. Then a freakish twist of the wind punctured a hole in the gray curtain, and I did see it.

"Well, Father Buliard, how does your new home look to you?"

The words came from my traveling companion, an older priest who had been to Coppermine many times. He had crowded into the space beside me. His eyes were laughing.

I laughed, too. I had to admit that the little town before us was no Paris. Coppermine is a lonely trading settlement on Coronation Gulf, an arm of the Arctic Ocean. It stands on the upper fringe of the mainland of Canada, looking north to the polar islands, north to the top of the world. No matter how you look at it, it is no thing of beauty. All I saw that morning, all there was to see, was a scattering of white frame houses along a high, white hill under a desolate white sky.

My companion had lifted his arm. He pointed out the buildings along the shore.

"That one," he said, "is the trading post of the Hudson's Bay Company. An old Scot runs it. Clean your ears before you meet him. He loves to talk.

"And that one . . ." He moved his arm. "That's where the Canadian weather experts work. I understand there's an American on the staff now."

His arm shifted again. This time there was no need to tell me the name of the building at which he was pointing. I had already spotted the little cross on the cupola above the sheet-iron roof and the statue of our Lord over the entryway below.

The cross . . . the figure of Christ . . . standing here on what seemed to be the very brink of the world! My throat filled. I turned away, wondering how soon the tears in my eyes would freeze in these chilling winds.

"There now," my companion was saying.

"You've had your first glimpse of Coppermine. Pretty dreary, eh?"

Yes, pretty dreary. But what did I care? I was happy! Here, at Coppermine, at the little chapel of Our Lady of Light, I could begin the work I had been longing to do—the work of a mission priest among the Eskimos of the Arctic Circle.

2. "DON'T FORGET TO SCRATCH!"

My arrival at Coppermine, Canada, was the climax of a venture that had started eight years before in 1926. I was then a youth of seventeen, going to the Christian Brothers' school in Besançon, France.

The brothers wanted me to learn Latin verbs. Like many lads my age, I preferred to daydream.

Most of my dreams dealt with what I would do when I grew up. According to a family legend, my ancestors had been daring fellows. "They were men who loved God—and enjoyed a good fight," I remember Papa saying. Some, he told me, had gone to the Crusades. Others had fought in the Hundred Years' War under the banners of the French king, John II, called John the Good. What could I do, I often wondered, that would not seem tame in comparison?

I found the answer, one sunny afternoon, in a downtown store. Idling along, daydreaming as usual, my eye was caught by the colorful jacket of a book in the store window.

I pressed my nose against the glass. The jacket pictured an Eskimo, as broad as he was tall in his caribou-skin parka and fur-lined hood. He stood alone on a seemingly endless plain covered with snow and ice.

Somehow, the picture set my blood to dancing. It spoke of adventure, of great deeds. I fingered the few francs in my pocket. A second later, I was inside the store. The clerk had my weekly allowance. I had the book.

It was called *The White Epic*. Its author, a French newspaperman, described a journey he had made through Eskimoland. He described the life of the natives and the work being carried on among them by a handful of mission priests belonging to an order called the Oblate Fathers of Mary Immaculate.

The Oblates! I rolled the word around on my tongue. That evening, at the supper table, I announced, "Mama, if they'll have me, I'm going to join the Oblates."

"The Oblates!" Mama's eyes shot heavenward before she turned them on Papa. "You hear!" she cried, her voice quivering with happiness. "We are going to have a priest in the family. A priest!"

I smiled to myself. Yes, I was going to be a priest—an Oblate—and, God willing, a missionary to the Eskimos.

I'd never been much of a student. To tell the truth, I did my best work on the playing field, or in the woods—a hunting rifle in hand. But, after reading *The White Epic*, I forced myself to study. I worked hard during my four years in the Oblate novitiate, even harder during another year at the seminary in Liége, Belgium.

At length, the great day came. One morning in 1934, at Le Havre, France, I said good-by to my family. I was on my way to the New World.

In Canada, my first important stop was at Fort Smith, a sandy riverside town in the wilderness of the Northwest Territories. There

I reported to Bishop Gabriel Breynat, my superior.

I stood humbly in the tall bishop's presence. His name was not new to me. I had encountered it many times in the pages of *The White Epic*, the book that had prompted me to become an Oblate.

Bishop Breynat was a Frenchman like myself. He had been a sickly youth. His doctors had sent him to Canada to die, but he had fooled them. When I met him, he had been a missionary to the Eskimos for fifty years. He had survived the toughest experiences the Arctic can offer. Once, on a long missionary journey, the toes of both feet had been frozen. Gangrene had set in. An Oblate brother, traveling with him, had amputated the toes with a pocketknife—without anesthetic, of course.

I spent a day and a night with him. During our final conversation, I said, "Your Lordship, before I start my work up north, can you give me any advice?"

"Why, yes," was the prompt reply. "When you go outdoors, put on your mittens."

We enjoyed a little chuckle together. Then suddenly the bishop's heavily lined face was serious.

"Father Buliard," he said, "you are about to carry the word of God to the Eskimos, the people living at the very top of the world."

He leaned toward me, speaking in a low voice. "You have a hard job on your hands," he said. "It will be easier if you remember one thing: no Eskimo will listen to you unless you first win his respect. And no Eskimo will respect you until you show him that you can do everything he can do—and that you can do it just as well."

Those words traveled north with me—north down 1,300 miles of the Mackenzie River, north and east through 700 miles of the Arctic Ocean to Coppermine.

When I recall my first months at Coppermine, I have to laugh. What a greenhorn I was! What an enormous lot I had to learn. As the bishop had said, a missionary cannot just live *with* the Eskimos; he must learn to live *like* them. He must learn to do what they do, eat what they eat. To some extent, he must even learn to think as they think.

The first job was to learn the language.

Then I knew only my own language—French. Today I know two other languages—Eskimo and English, which I learned after reaching Coppermine. Believe me, French and English are child's play compared with the language spoken by the little people of the frozen north. You can get along nicely if you know a thousand English words. To speak Eskimo fluently, you have to know fifteen thousand. The grammar is tough, too. As for the pronunciation, well—try this one trippingly on the tongue:

Krinrarkratakreaotigivaktuksagaluaraptigo.

It is a single Eskimo word. In English it takes a whole sentence to say, for it means roughly, "We should pray more often to God."

All my life I had been a good hunter and fisherman. That is, I thought I was good until I saw how the Eskimos went about it. In short order, I had to learn how to jiggle fish out of the ocean by dropping a line through thick ice. I had to learn the tricks of tracking down the hard-to-find caribou, the shaggy reindeer which travels in herds and lives by grazing on the green moss growing under the Arctic snows.

I had to learn how to build a snowhouse in ninety minutes flat. Anyone who takes longer, according to the Eskimos, is an "ignoramus, too dumb for words."

I had to learn how to build a dog sled, how to drive it, how to harness and manage the thick-coated Husky dogs who pull it.

And, of course, I had to learn how to keep

alive outdoors in an empty and roadless land where, in order to visit two or three friends, you often have to travel by dog sled between two hundred and a thousand miles.

Fortunately, I had good teachers. One of them was a rough and leathery Eskimo hunter whom we at the mission house had nicknamed Rawbones. I remember the rather warm June morning that Rawbones came around saying, "Falla perhaps would like to learn how to hunt Nathek in the spring."

Falla is as near as the Eskimos can come to pronouncing the word Father. Nathek is their name for the seal.

I nodded. "Yes, Rawbones," I said. "I should be delighted to learn. When does the lesson begin?"

I assumed, of course, that we would get the dogs and strike out at once for the ocean where Nathek, the seal, lives. But no! Rawbones kicked open the mission house door with his booted foot. He indicated that I was to enter.

"What kind of joke is this?" I asked. "There are no seals in here."

Rawbones' soft black eyes found mine. Since that day I have looked into the faces of a thousand Eskimos. I have yet to see one whose eyes were not just about to brim over with laughter. The rugged young hunter was no exception. He laughed a little, then a little more, and finally bent double in a roar.

When he had straightened up and got his breath, he said, "Falla, when an Eskimo asks you for baptism, do you get the cup at once and splash water on him?"

"Of course not. He has to be instructed first."

"Exactly. And Falla must first be instructed before he goes out to hunt Nathek in the spring. Come!"

Rawbones planted himself on one of the hard benches in the mission house living room. His instructions went on and on. He took his time, I suspect, because we had a good brand of tea at the mission, and the Eskimos are even fonder of tea than the English are. As Rawbones started the lesson, I put on the kettle. I had refilled it many times before he finished.

On and on he talked, forming his words in the back of his throat the way Eskimos do. The words came out in little chugs like a pig grunting. On and on Rawbones talked, telling me about Nathek, the seal.

Nathek is important to the Eskimos. His meat is delicious eating. His hide is used to make men's trousers, parts of boats, dog sleds, and a dozen other things. Most important is his blubber—his fat. Nathek's blubber is the Eskimos' fuel. They use it in the hollowed-out stone lamps that both heat and light their winter igloos.

When winter comes, a pack of ice, sometimes six feet deep, roofs the churning Arctic Ocean. Then, of course, Nathek must live in the watery depths. He is not a fish, however. He is a mammal. Occasionally he needs a breath of air. To get it, he drills half a dozen cone-shaped breathing holes through the ice. He scoops them out with his long-nailed flippers.

The Eskimos' name for Nathek's breathing hole is *aglu*. At the surface, the *aglu* is only an inch or two wide. But that is room enough for Nathek. He can poke his whiskered snout through and get his quota of air.

Obviously, it is no trick to catch a seal in the winter. One needs only a rifle or a harpoon and a little patience. True, snow often hides the seal's breathing holes. Very well; bring the dogs along. They will sniff them out fast enough.

Then all you have to do is stand and wait. Pretty soon a hissing sound at the *aglu* tells you that Nathek is there. Then—crack! goes your rifle; or—zoom! goes your harpoon; and Nathek is on his way to the igloo. There the women of the family will finish butchering him, and the neighbors will drop in that evening for a seal-meat banquet.

There are days, of course, when the wind screams across the ice and you can't hear Nathek's breathing. The Eskimos have a solution for that. They place in the *aglu* a piece of bone like a thick knitting needle. When Nathek comes up for air, he has to push out the bone, thus warning the hunter of his presence.

Personally, I have never taken to this kind of seal hunting. I haven't the Eskimos patience. To stand out on the ice, acting as a backstop for the cold wind and waiting, waiting . . . What a waste of time! Then, too, it's not very sporting. Once Nathek shoves his black head through the breathing hole, how can you miss? He is then a sure target.

But hunting Nathek in the spring when the ice begins to break—ah! As Rawbones pointed out during our lesson in the mission house, that is a different matter. That is an art, a skill. It is a true sport.

Nathek likes to get his summer tan early. The minute the ice starts to waste away under the spring sun, he finds a thin spot and cracks through. Up and down he bobs, up and down. He does this several times, looking all around to make sure neither of his enemies—the Eskimo hunter or the big polar bear—is in the neighborhood.

Satisfied that all is safe, he picks out a cozy island of solid ice, clambers onto it, and stretches out for a snooze in the sun.

Then, you say, why not just walk out on the ice and shoot him? It is not so simple as that. Nathek is no fool. He doesn't sleep long at a time. He cat naps. Every few seconds, he lifts his head and looks carefully around. On the open ice, he can spy you long before you can get near enough to shoot him. When he does see you, back into the water he plops, out of sight and gun range.

So how do you get near enough to shoot him? "You outsmart him!" I remember Rawbones shouting at me during our mission house session. "You make him believe that you are a seal yourself."

"How?"

The Eskimo hunter met my question with a wild fling of his arms. "You drop face down on the ice and crawl toward him; that's how," he cried. "You don't crawl straight. You crawfish, wriggling this way and that, the way a seal crawls. You crawl as long as Nathek sleeps. When he wakes up and looks around, you stop. Only . . . !"

Rawbones' index finger came up to my face

in a warning gesture. "Only," he repeated with emphasis, "don't make the mistake of lying stock still."

He waved his finger in my face again and repeated, "Don't lie still! Nathek never lies still for long. If you do, he'll know you're no seal. You must lift your head every so often and look around the way he does. You must arrange your arms to look like flippers. Above all, you must . . ."

But I won't tell you right now the other thing you must do. I'll tell you only that when Rawbones finally completed his instructions and we went out on the sea ice, I forgot to do it. As a result, a funny thing happened—with the joke, of course, on me.

We didn't take the dogs. The ice near the shore was rubbery and unsafe. It swayed under our weight as we proceeded cautiously, testing it from time to time with our harpoons.

Suddenly my companion stood still. I did the same.

"Nathek?" I asked.

Rawbones nodded. His eyes, sharpened by a lifetime in the shadow of the North Pole, had spotted a lone seal. The seal was sunning himself on the ice alongside a crack of open water. The big, black, gleaming fellow lay about three hundred yards away. I would have to crawl about a hundred and fifty yards to get a good shot at his head.

Rawbones had squatted behind a hummock of snow. "Now do it right, Falla," I heard him call to me. "Let's see if you remember my instructions."

I was already face down on the ice, crawling forward. I was determined to get that seal. I knew the penalty if I didn't. An Eskimo loves to get the laugh on a white man. If I failed to bag a seal this afternoon, I knew what Rawbones would do. He would spend the evening going from friend to friend, telling them what a fool Falla had made of himself out on the ice.

I wriggled along fast, splashing through shallow pools of water. When Nathek awakened and lifted his head, I halted. Now, I knew, was the test. Could I fool him? Could I make old Nathek think I was just another seal snoozing on the ice? "Crook your arms and flap them like flippers," Rawbones had told me. I did so. "Lift your head at intervals and look around." I did that, too.

Even at this distance, I could feel the seal's eyes trained directly on me. I could imagine what was going on in his little head. "Is that a friend or a foe?" he was asking himself. "Is it another seal—or a hunter?"

He started to lower his head. I was beginning to think I had fooled him when suddenly he was gone! There was a quick movement as he slithered into the water and disappeared.

I jumped to my feet, feeling silly and shouting, "What did I do wrong? Now what did I do wrong?"

Rawbones came running. He was laughing. "You forgot something, Falla."

"On the contrary, I remembered everything you told me."

"Everything but the lice!"

The lice! Oh yes, the lice! Nathek, the seal, is troubled with lice, especially in the spring when he is shedding hair. Naturally, when he comes up to sun-bathe, he scratches himself often and vigorously. My failure to do so had given me away.

"Never mind, Falla." Rawbones was still laughing. "We will see many more seals before the day is done—only, next time, don't forget to scratch!"

3. BLOODY FALLS

Twenty-one years have passed since I went out on the sea ice with Rawbones and shot, or rather, missed, my first seal. I have bagged many since. I have hunted with many Eskimos. Naturally, I have learned a few things about the little people of the Arctic. Before introducing them, however, I must tell you about the first Catholic priests ever to work among them.

To us Arctic Long Robes, as the Eskimos call us, the story of Father Rouvière and Father

LeRoux is an inspiring one. It is a story of faith, of courage—and of murder.

Today, there are five busy Catholic missions along the 15,000-mile Arctic coast. In 1910, there were none. The nearest church was below the Arctic Circle in a Mackenzie River village called Fort Good Hope. There Father Rouvière, a young French Oblate, was preaching and working with two Canadian Indian tribes.

One day, near the village, Father Rouvière saw a group of men far different in appearance from his Indians. They had slanted eyes and yellow skin. They were heavily wrapped in furs. Their faces, outlined by peaked hoods trimmed with wolverine, had the shape of footballs. Their guttural language reminded Father Rouvière of German, and they smiled and laughed a great deal.

"Who are these cheerful fellows?" he asked an Indian friend.

"Neighbors of ours," the tribesman replied. "They live in the Barren Land along the Arctic Ocean. Recently they have been coming south to trade with us."

"And what do you call them?"

The Indian shrugged. "*Eskimeow*," was his answer.

Eskimeow is an Algonquin Indian word. It means "they eat their meat raw."

Through an interpreter, Father Rouvière talked with some of the Eskimos themselves. "Have any of you," he asked, "ever heard of our Lord, Jesus Christ?"

"Our Lord . . . Jesus . . . ?" The Eskimos looked blankly at one another and even more blankly at Father Rouvière.

A few months later, Father Rouvière left his comfortable mission house in Fort Good Hope. He had been ordered by his bishop to travel north, to find the Eskimos, to set up a mission among them.

He started out in midsummer. Taking only his portable chapel, some tools, and a few provisions, he paddled his canoe 165 miles across Great Bear Lake to Dease Bay. There the Eskimos were supposed to be encamped. But Father Rouvière was too late. The Eskimos had gone north to their winter hunting grounds.

Father Rouvière followed. When the going got too rough by water, he abandoned his canoe. Back-packing his supplies, he trudged on. Soon he was beyond what is called the tree line, in the rock-strewn wastes of Eskimoland itself.

He had assumed, when he started, that he would quickly overtake the hunters. He found out otherwise. For forty days he traveled without seeing a single person. He was beginning to think he never would. Then, one morning, near a lake which now bears his name, Father Rouvière sighted three black specks against a distant hill.

He leaned forward under his heavy pack. "Are those wolves?" he wondered. "Or caribou, perhaps? Or . . . ?"

He straightened up, a prayer of thanks on his lips. It was Assumption Day, August 15, 1911. "Our Blessed Lady," he told himself, "has smiled on her Oblate!"

The three specks were Eskimo hunters. They hurried forward. When they were close enough to see Father Rouvière, they clasped their hands above their heads in the traditional Eskimo gesture of greeting and welcome. Father Rouvière rushed toward them, shouting in their language the few words he had managed to learn.

He spent the next winter on the banks of what is now Lake Rouvière. He built a log cabin and set up his portable chapel. He studied the Eskimo language. He preached to the hunters who now and then drifted through the area. He made a few converts to Christianity.

In the summer of 1912, he was joined by another Oblate, twenty-seven-year-old Father LeRoux. Together they made plans.

"We are located too far south," Father

Rouvière pointed out. "The Eskimos hunt here off and on, but they do not stay. If we are to make many converts, we had better settle where more of them actually live."

After further conferences, the priests decided to move to Coppermine, some 300 miles away on the shores of the Arctic Sea. A small band of Eskimo hunters waved them off. At the turn of the trail, the young Oblates stopped and waved back. Then they headed into the northern wastelands—and disappeared.

What happened to them? For three years nobody had the slightest idea. In Fort Smith the bishop shook his head sadly. "I'm afraid," he said, "that the fathers never reached Coppermine. They must have perished on the trail."

Living in Coppermine in 1914 was an American explorer. At a festival in a snow dance hall one night, his eye was caught by the strange appearance of some Eskimo hunters. One was wearing a cassock over his parka. The others had decked themselves with the tattered remnants of what had once been priestly vestments.

The explorer said nothing to the Eskimos. He reported what he had seen to the bishop in Fort Smith. The bishop, in turn, notified the Royal Canadian Mounted Police. The following year a patrol of constables arrived at Coppermine.

The police officers questioned the Eskimos cautiously. At first they learned nothing. Then one of the officers had a bright idea which he passed on to the interpreter. "Ask the Eskimos straight out," he said, "who killed the two priests."

On the heels of this direct question, the whole story came to light. Fathers Rouvière and LeRoux had not perished on their way to Coppermine, as the bishop had suspected. They had reached the settlement, all right. They had built a church. They had taught the Eskimos and won some converts. All had gone well until the Eskimos began arguing among themselves. Some said the Long Robes had brought bad luck to the country and that they should be killed or, at least, sent away.

In time, the arguments grew into open fights. Not wishing to be the cause of bloodshed, the Oblates decided to move elsewhere.

On the day of their departure, both were sick. They had to move slowly on the trail. Toward noon, two young Eskimos from Coppermine caught up with them. The Eskimos pretended to be friendly, but that night they killed the priests in their sleep and made off with their belongings.

Thus, far from their French homes, Fathers Rouvière and LeRoux laid down their lives for

God. Their bodies were never found. Their empty graves lie on the hillside where they were killed. I have been to the site many times. It overlooks a deep and rocky gorge of the Coppermine River. Its name on modern maps is Bloody Falls.

When news of the deaths of Fathers Rouvière and LeRoux was made known, every priest in the Northwest Territories clamored to be sent north in their place.

The first to go died within a few months—frozen in an Arctic lake. The second was Father Pierre Fallaise, a great priest who was to become one of my close friends in later years.

Father Fallaise worked alone for years in the vicinity of Lake Rouvière. He did not have an easy time of it. The Eskimos taunted him. Over and over they reminded him of what had happened to Fathers Rouvière and LeRoux.

"What if we did the same to you?" a young Eskimo asked him one day.

"We are not afraid to kill Long Robes," another said. "Suppose we kill you?"

Father Fallaise answered them with a smile. He spoke to them of God, calling Him the "Great Good Spirit." The Eskimos laughed in his face.

He said Mass in a crude log cabin. In a big tent next door, the shaman—the Eskimo medicine man—held a noisy session, drowning out the Father's voice.

He nursed the sick. He had some medical skill and effected many cures. Often, however, he would no sooner leave a patient's tent than the shaman would take his place. Sometimes the shaman would strangle the sick Eskimo, saying, "This is what you get for seeking the aid of a Long Robe!"

As Father Fallaise passed through the Eskimo camp, angry glances followed him.

"You are not wanted here. You are an intruder," the people called after him.

"Go away," they cried. "Leave us, or prepare yourself to die."

Father Fallaise smiled—and stayed on.

The years passed. Some of the Eskimos shook their heads in wonder. "The Falla," they said, "must have a secret charm that protects him. He must have some powerful medicine." Others had to admire the priest's courage. Now and then they slipped into his cabin to hear Mass. Some became Christians.

When, in 1928, Father Fallaise left the area, his enemies laughed. "See," they said triumphantly, "he has no great magic after all. He has run away from us in fear."

The faithful ones smiled. "Oh, no," they said. "The Falla has only gone to get wood for a white man's house. He is going to start a new mission at Coppermine. He told us so himself, and he is a man who never lies."

They were right. At Herschell Island, near the coast of Alaska, Father Fallaise purchased an old schooner and loaded it with supplies. In August of 1928, the schooner sailed from Herschell bound east for Coppermine. Aboard were Father Fallaise and two other priests.

They were not to reach their destination that year. Caught in a fierce storm, they took refuge at Lettie Harbor, some 300 miles west of Coppermine. "Very well," Father Fallaise said, "since we can go no farther until next summer, we will set up a mission here."

They did, and what then seemed to be a setback turned out to be a great blessing. Today, almost all of the people living at Lettie Harbor are Christianized Eskimos.

The next year the mission at Coppermine was built with Father Fallaise in charge. In 1931, Father Fallaise left for Fort Smith, having been promoted to bishop and given the post of coadjutor to Bishop Breynat. Two years later, Father Delelande–the priest who would be my first superior in the northland–took over.

By the time I arrived in 1934, the Eskimos of Coppermine had become fairly sociable. I remember pleasant winter evenings, talking with them in the mission house. Groups often dropped in at dusk. They liked sitting around on the hard benches, making jokes and drinking tea. The women brought their babies. The men helped me with my language lessons. I would point to this object or that. They would tell me the Eskimo name for it, laughing uproariously when I made a mistake.

It seemed to me that I had never met a friendlier, or a more good-natured, group of people. Still, once in a while, a shudder would pass through me as I remembered the tragedy of Bloody Falls.

The Eskimos had not forgotten either. One evening, a dark-skinned native I had never met before took my hand and held it overlong. He looked hard into my eyes and grinned.

"Are you happy among us, Falla?" he asked.

"Why, of course," I replied.

"I am surprised."

"Why are you surprised?"

"Because, Falla, you are living with people who think nothing of killing Long Robes. Aren't you afraid?"

I told him, "No, of course I'm not afraid." I said it in a loud and hearty voice. But, during those early months among the Arctic savages, to tell the truth, I sometimes was!

4. INUK

Who are the Eskimos and where did they come from?

I cannot tell you about them all. I have not met all of the 40,000 yellow-skinned natives of Eskimoland.

Those I know best, my Eskimos, are the ones living in the vicinity of Coronation Gulf.

Years ago an explorer—the same explorer who helped track down the murderers of Fathers Rouvière and LeRoux—gave my people a name. He called them the Copper Eskimos because, before the white man came with his rifles and steel knives, my Eskimos made their weapons and tools out of the hunks of copper they found on the surface of the ground.

All Eskimos belong to the same race. They are a single people. In one way, however, the Copper Eskimos are different from the Eskimos living to the west of them in Alaska and from those in northeastern Canada and Greenland. They have had less to do with civilized men. They are more primitive. To this day my Eskimos live pretty much as all Eskimos lived before the white men came among them.

All Eskimos are proud. Their official name for themselves is not Eskimo. They call themselves Inuit, pronounced ee-noo-it. Inuit is an Eskimo word meaning "the men."

Ask any Eskimo man anywhere, "Who are you?"

His reply is prompt and proud. "I am Inuk!" he declares.

Inuk, pronounced ee-nuk, is an Eskimo word meaning "THE man."

Inuk is THE man because the Eskimos, as they see it, are the only real men on earth. Their name for the Indians living south of them below the tree line is Irk-rel-ret, meaning the Lice. Since Eskimos rarely have eyebrows and white men almost always do, their name for the white man is Krab-loo-nak, meaning "the Big Eyebrows."

And, according to the Eskimos, the average Big Eyebrows is an ignoramus, a stupid fellow.

There is no use arguing with them about it.

"Come now," I recall saying to my good Eskimo friend Rawbones, "confess that we white men are good for something. After all, you like our guns, and it is we who invented them."

"True," Rawbones replied haughtily, "but before you came with your guns, we had our harpoons. And we caught just as much game with them."

"But the radio, the 'voice of the wind,' as you call it," I insisted. "Admit now that you enjoy listening to the radio. Again, it is we who invented it."

"The radio," Rawbones conceded, "is very pleasant—so long as the weather is good. When the winds and the storms come, your radio is all static, and it only hurts the ears."

I was not licked yet. "How about the great bird, the airplane?" I demanded. "Is that not a wonderful invention?"

"Wonderful," Rawbones nodded, "so long as it remains in the air. But I hear that they often fall down!"

There's no use going on. Say what you will about the white man and his inventions, the Eskimo continues to think of himself as Inuk, THE man! He has reason to. After all, his is a country where almost nothing grows, a country which outsiders speak of as the Barren Land. Inuk keeps happy and cheerful and healthy in a country where, according to him, the Indians (those lice!) and the stupid Big Eyebrows would only starve and die!

Inuk has no written history, no recorded past. Like the people of every land, the Eskimos sing songs about the good old days. But you can listen to their songs all night and all day, and still not know much about the Eskimos' past, for the songs are mostly myths and fairy tales.

In recent years, however, some white men—a group of Big Eyebrows calling themselves ethnologists—have carefully studied the Eskimos. Today, these students agree that the Eskimos did not always live in North America.

Long ago, probably many centuries before the days of our Lord, the Eskimos lived in northern China. They were Mongolians, an Oriental people.

Once, long ago indeed, the Eskimos left northern China. Why? One guess is that their land was invaded by powerful enemies pouring in from the south. Anyhow, they moved north, through Mongolia and across Siberia. On and on they trekked, until one day they could go no farther. They had reached the sea!

What a wail must have gone up from many thousand Eskimo throats that day. "The Great Water!" one can imagine them crying out in horror. "The salt!"

They were standing on the shores of Bering Strait. A weaker people might have given up then and there. They might have just sat down, letting their pursuing enemies overtake and conquer them.

Not the Eskimos; not the Inuit. Bering Strait is a part of the sea, all right, but it is only sixty miles wide. For eight months of the year it freezes solid, forming a natural bridge between Asia and America, between Siberia and Alaska. So the Inuit walked across. Like the Israelites fleeing from Egypt, they crossed water, hoping to find for themselves a Promised Land.

How disappointed they must have been when they reached the other side! All that lay before them was snow and ice, and still more snow and ice.

So they dipped south, and one day they stopped again. This time their shout was a shout of joy.

They had sighted the tree line. Ahead of them lay the spreading forests of Canada.

What could be more wonderful! In the forests, they could live secure and happy. In the forests, they could find fuel for heat and light, wood for homes, wild animals and birds for food.

But when they reached the forest, they found that some had preceded them to the North American continent—the Indians!

The Indians did not want to share their hunting grounds with a horde of odd-looking immigrants and foreigners. Hastily they assembled around their blazing council fires.

"These people on our borders," they grunted, "are not like us. They do not look like us or act like us. They are not nice and refined. They are savages. We must keep them out!"

So there was a war. The Indians had all the advantages. They fought from established camps. Over the years they had developed a class of professional warriors—an army.

The Eskimos had come to the end of their journey. They dared not enter the forests to be killed by the Indians. They dared not return to Asia to be conquered by their enemies there. They had to stay where they were. Somehow, some way, they had to learn how to live in the Barren Land, in the vast white desert of the Arctic.

5. LOST ON THE TRAIL

Actually, the Arctic desert is not always white. At times, the nine-month winter seems endless. But, eventually, it does end. Spring comes, and, after it, a short summer and an even shorter fall.

Here, in the land of the Copper Eskimos, there are about twelve hours of sunlight on March 21. After that, the days lengthen steadily until the beginning of May. For the next three months, the sun never leaves the sky.

Three months of endless daylight! Then, little by little, the night returns. By the end of November, there is nothing but night. For two months, the Eskimos go to bed and get up by moonlight. Sometimes the northern lights (the aurora borealis) sweep the sky with flapping draperies of flame. Otherwise, the only illumination is a pale glimmer along the horizon like the glow above an open-air arena.

During the long, dark winter, the sea is frozen. Sea and land become one. With the return of daylight, the sea begins to open. Most of the snow slowly disappears. The tundra, as the crusty soil of Eskimoland is called, comes to view.

There is something startling about the Arctic spring. Suddenly you are aware of the scent of flowers, wafted on breezes that only yesterday were like floating icicles. For a brief period flowers dot the land: bluebells, poppies, hundreds of others. They spring up between the rocks and poke through lingering patches of snow. Birds twitter, green grass sprouts, and the brooks and lakes become a deep blue.

As the days grow longer, the flowers wither and die. The grass becomes brown. The brooks dry up, and the lakes turn slate gray. Until winter returns with its deep blanket of snow, the steppes—as the Arctic plains are called—

look forlorn and burnt-out. Not even a shrub is to be seen. There is nothing anywhere but colorless lichen and spongy moss; nothing but the rock-strewn tundra; nothing but deep gullies and jagged cliffs, whose stony walls exhibit every imaginable color, including black, gray, red, green, and even pure white.

In this uncomfortable land, Inuk—THE man—passes his days. He is always on the go. Never ask Inuk for his address. He has none, or, at any rate, he never has one for long. The animals and fish on which he depends will not come to him, so he must go to them. Consequently, Inuk is a perpetual hunter, an everlasting fisherman. He is a wanderer, a nomad.

In winter, Inuk usually hunts and fishes alone. He leaves his snow igloo in the morning and returns to it at night. In summer, he often takes the family along.

It is something to see—an Eskimo family trudging across the tundra on a blinding-bright summer day. Leading the little caravan is Inuk himself, THE man, the family ruler. As he tramps proudly along, his eyes search the surrounding flats, always on the alert for game.

There are many things to be carried, but Inuk carries only three: his hunting knife, his rifle, and his ammunition. Behind him, in single file, come the children, each carrying a few small objects. Last of all comes his wife, bowed double under a bulging pack. The pack is held to her forehead by a sealskin strap. It is filled with oil pots, fur clothes, and cooking utensils. Close to the woman (is it not she who feeds them?) run the scraggly dogs, straining under their overloaded packs.

For a month, two months, sometimes longer, the Eskimo family may live thus on the trail. They often cover hundreds and hundreds of miles. Eskimos are born to such travel. They think nothing of it. But a white man, new to the country—well! I can laugh now over my first summer trip in 1935, but it wasn't entirely funny at the time.

My destination was a camp on Dismal Lake, 150 miles from Coppermine. I should say "our" destination. My Eskimo friend Rawbones made the journey with me.

We had a little chat before setting forth.

"Now, Falla," my friend grunted, "I have never been to Dismal Lake. I cannot guide you."

"Think nothing of it," I told him. "Dismal Lake is directly south and west, and it is a large body of water. How could we miss it?"

Rawbones gave me a sharp look. I had a faint suspicion that he was laughing at me, but I wasn't sure. All he said was, "We *could* miss it, Falla!"

There was a compass at the mission house. Today I wouldn't dream of striking into the wilds without one. But I was young, then, and a smart aleck. As we made our preparations for what I thought was going to be a pleasant little walk, I never gave the compass a thought.

We started in the early morning, taking three dogs to pack our supplies. We needed the dogs, also, to carry back the meat in case we met, and got a shot at, a herd of caribou.

The first day wasn't bad. Our only real difficulty was the mosquitoes. In the Arctic winter, the worst thing you can meet on the trail is a blizzard. In summer, the worst thing is the mosquitoes. They swoop on you in swarms. After an hour among them, your face is a swollen and throbbing pulp.

As we walked along, swatting at them, Rawbones said, "Falla, did you bring the tent?"

"No, I didn't."

"But don't you remember my telling you . . . ?"

"I remember," I said rather impatiently. "You told me to bring a tent, but I saw no point in carrying a lot of extra weight. It's only a short trip, and there are no signs of rain."

Another sharp look from Rawbones. Another grunted warning. "It *could* rain," he said.

It did. It rained that night. It poured. In fact,

it poured every night throughout the journey.

On the third morning I awakened drenched to the skin, as usual. Rawbones was already on his feet. I can see him yet—running toward me across the soggy plain, bellowing like a hungry calf.

"Falla! Falla! The dogs. Two of them are gone!"

We searched all over the place, but there were no two ways about it. The dogs were gone. With them had gone the packs we had strapped to their bodies. Those packs, alas, contained all our food!

Fortunately, the pack on the remaining dog held a primus stove. Fortunately, too, the night's rain had deposited an ample supply of water in the deep holes which riddle the northern tundra. I gathered some water in a trading store basin. Rawbones gathered some moss and ground it into a powder. The water and the moss, heated together on the primus stove, gave us a breakfast of tea, real Eskimo style.

"Be of good cheer," I said as we started the day's trek. "We'll kill our lunch along the way. We're bound to see some animal to shoot at."

Again Rawbones' sharp look. And once again his dubious grunt. "You know, Falla," he said, "we *could* see nothing at all."

For many hours we didn't. What we most

hoped to see was a herd of caribou, for the meat of the North American reindeer is delicious. But noon came, and still we had spotted nothing. We trudged on, our steps lagging, our stomachs shrinking—and shrieking—with hunger. By mid-afternoon, I was saying to myself:

"If only we could spot just one Arctic hare."

In fact, I would have gladly settled for a mouthful of the chipmunk-like ground squirrel the Eskimos call Siksik because "sik! sik!" is the noise he makes.

After the rain, it was a fine day, full of sparkle. Dainty cloud shadows raced across the steppes. Overhead was a clear sky, and nothing is more beautiful than the clear sky of the Arctic.

Toward evening the landscape suddenly altered for the worse. A sickly gray fell over it as the sun slid behind a cloud.

"More rain tonight," Rawbones remarked gloomily. "A hard one, I would guess, from the looks of . . ."

He halted. I halted.

Standing on a near-by hill was a lone caribou, magnificent to see. A fine bull, his spread antlers pierced the dulling sky.

He was a big fellow. At a reasonable distance, say 400 yards, he would be almost a sure hit.

I squinted, trying to estimate the yardage between us. A walk of about 200 yards up the hill, I figured, would bring me close enough.

"I'll get him," I told Rawbones. "That's a rough hill, and I have the younger legs."

Rawbones grunted assent. Wobbly with hunger, he was perfectly content to rest on a convenient boulder and watch me work.

Stalking a caribou is not the same as stalking Nathek, the seal. There's no point in getting down and crawling along as fast as you can. The noise you'd make as you displaced rocks would have Mr. Caribou showing you his hoofs in a moment. Your best bet is to proceed in various ways. Crawl a little, but slowly. Get to your feet. Step ahead, slowly. When Mr. Caribou gives you the eye, stop dead still. Seeing you against the gray day, he may mistake your brown parka for a shadow across the landscape.

Creep . . . walk . . . stop. Creep . . . walk . . . stop. The 200 yards, traversed in this manner, seemed like 100 miles.

Finally, I was in what seemed to be a good position. I shouldered my rifle. All was set when——

"Yow-l-l-l-l-l-l-l!"

"*Sapristi!*" The old French slang word escaped me.

Our one remaining dog would have to let out a yelp at this moment!

I lifted my sights and fired wildly. The caribou bull responded with a leap that put a foot of sky between his hoofs and the earth.

Then he was gone.

I relaxed, only to become tense again as I heard Rawbones scrabbling up the hill behind me. He was shouting.

"You hit him, Falla. Come! Let's pursue!"

We were up that incline and over it in no time. Sure enough! I could see from the way the bull was running that I had nicked him. Even so, he gave us a breathless chase. It took the two of us, shooting madly, to bring him down.

What a supper we had! There was no waiting for the oven to heat, either. I had been in the Arctic long enough to prefer my meat raw, which is the Eskimo way. The Inuit would rather have it frozen, but beggars cannot be choosers. Out on the Arctic tundra in the nightless summer, without a deepfreezer to our name, we couldn't be fussy.

We gorged ourselves. Then we piled a circle of big stones around what remained of our caribou to protect it from the wolves. After that, we crawled into our fur sleeping bags and fell sound asleep—to the march-like patter of rain, of course, for our nightly downpour had arrived on schedule.

When I awakened, some hours later, the rain had stopped. But an even more horrible sound filled the night. It came from about fifty feet away, where I could see Rawbones cruelly beating our one dog. He was beating and cursing. (And I must tell you that Eskimos do not swear like troopers; they swear like Eskimos, which is considerably worse.) I ran over, horrified. But I was too late. The dog was dead.

As I started to protest, Rawbones pointed to a sorry sight on the ground. I saw what had happened. The dog had eaten the rest of our caribou. Nothing remained but a heap of highly polished bones!

Breakfast the next morning was moss tea, scalding hot!

As we consumed it, Rawbones brought up a matter that had been troubling us both. "Falla," he said, "we have been on the trail many days. How far would you say we have come?"

I knew what thought was running through his mind. We should have reached the shores of Dismal Lake by this time. We were lost—hopelessly lost!

"Rawbones," I said, "my foolishness got us

into this. Now let me have a sample of your wisdom. What do you suggest we do?"

"Go home. We will never find Dismal Lake, but if we head north, we're bound to hit the sea and Coppermine."

It took us three days. We found no more game. It was three days on a diet of moss tea. As we stumbled into the mission house yard, some little Eskimo children came running out. At the sight of our faces, they stopped in astonishment.

The mosquitoes had really done a job on us. Our faces were swollen like overblown balloons. Our eyes must have looked like deep tunnels. For many miles, on the return journey, we had had to cross a field still covered with snow. Each of us had a bad case of sun blindness. This makes your eyes feel as if someone had blown sand into them—a miserable feeling.

The darkness of the mission house was a blessed relief. I changed my clothes, drank a little hot broth, and fell into a short, but welcome, sleep.

When I awakened, one of my colleagues, a young Oblate brother, dropped a little kerosene into my tortured eyes. Kerosene is the Inuit's remedy for sun blindness. It doesn't soothe right away. On the contrary, it brings on a new pain so sharp that you forget the pain of the sun blindness. In a short time, all distress goes, and you feel like a human being again.

Before he left to rejoin his family, Rawbones, too, got a snooze and a dose of kerosene for his eyes. We were both mighty happy to be home again. As for me, I had learned a lesson. I respect the difficulties of the trail now. Even on a short journey, I have no objections to carrying a little extra weight. I take along all the supplies one might possibly require—plus a compass!

6. RAWBONES' WINTER HOME

During the short Arctic summer, my Eskimos live in tents made of caribou skin. Outside each tent, a low fire, smoldering between flat rocks, keeps the teakettle warm. Except for driftwood floating in from the sea, there is no timber around. The fire is fed with a dried moss very much like the peat used on the hearthstones of Ireland.

When the days shorten and the thermometer starts its gradual slide toward 60° below zero,

Inuk puts up his winter home, his snow igloo. You may wonder why I say snow igloo, instead of just igloo. The reason is that to the Eskimo any home is an igloo, whether it be made of snow, wood, sod, or caribou skin.

As a rule, Inuk builds his winter home on the coast of the frozen sea. The sea is the home of Nathek, the seal, whose blubber feeds the stone lamps of the igloo. It is the home, too, of many of the fish that make up the bulk of Inuk's winter diet. Most important of all, traveling is easier on the sea ice. There are no hills to climb, no great gullies to cross.

Late one fall, the Eskimo Nip-a-la-ri-ok and his family decided to erect their winter house right out on the sea ice.

Rawbones advised them against it. "The ice is not firm yet, Nipalariok," he said. "Suddenly you may find 100 yards of open water between yourselves and the shore."

"Oh, nothing will happen to us," Nipalariok said.

But something did happen. A few days later, Nipalariok and his family awakened to find that the ice on which their house rested had separated from the surrounding ice. They were adrift on a floating island.

At noon I hurried down to the beach. I stood there with a group of Inuit, watching the Nipalarioks sail swiftly by. We could see Nipalariok and his family standing in front of their igloo, waving at us. We waved back. A few hours later they glided over the horizon and out of sight.

For three days they drifted. Eighty miles off land, they ran into luck. The ocean current shifted, bringing them back. Late the following evening, they were once again within sight of the coast. During the night, the open water between their island and the shore ice froze over. The next morning, the Nipalarioks loaded their belongings on the family sled and came safely ashore.

"Weren't you frightened?" I asked Nipalariok afterward.

His answer was a shrug. "*Pirtok!*" he said.

Pirtok is a favorite Eskimo word meaning: Nothing—one can do nothing about it.

It sums up the Inuit's philosophy. Inuk never bothers his head about tomorrow. He never complains. If things go well, he laughs and sings. If they go badly, he shrugs.

"*Pirtok!*" he says. "Nothing—one can do nothing about it."

One week the hunting and fishing are good. His larder full, Inuk rushes to the door of his igloo and shouts, "*Nek-re-to-rit-se!* Come and eat!" That night, he stuffs himself and all his neighbors with a great feast. Next week, no fish come to his net; no bird or animal comes within range of his rifle sights. Starvation threatens. Does Inuk worry? Not at all. He shrugs.

"*Pirtok!*" he says. "Nothing—one can do nothing about it!"

Building the snow igloo is an art. These days I can toss one together pretty snappily, thanks to Rawbones. He was my teacher, and a good one.

"Come," he said, one crackling fall morning, "I am going to build my house. You will watch. Perhaps you will learn how to do it."

As we ran with the dogs alongside the sled, "*Perhaps* you will learn," he repeated with emphasis. "After all, no Big Eyebrows can ever build a snow house the way Inuk can."

We traveled a mile or so to where a number of Eskimos had decided to place their winter camp. They had chosen a level area near the frozen sea. A few houses were already up. Each rose some six to ten feet above the snow line, its rounded sides and domed roof glistening in the sun.

Rawbones cracked his seventy-foot walrus-hide whip over the heads of his nine dogs. "March!" he shouted as we both hopped aboard the sledge to descend the final hill. "Gee! To the right! Haw! To the left! Ho! Stop!"

We had arrived. A few minutes later, Rawbones was hard at it. I followed his every move.

Inuk loves flattery. "Wonderful!" I said to Rawbones every so often. "It's amazing how you do it!"

Every time he gave me the same answer. "It is nothing," he snorted. "This house will not be as good as my other ones. It is early in the season, and the snow is not very good yet."

The snow, of course, must be just right: not too hard, not too soft. Rawbones' first job was to find the proper snow. For some time he prodded here and there, using the Eskimos' main building tool—a saber-like knife made out of caribou antler.

"Ah!" he said at length. "This isn't bad."

He began to build. First, he drew a large and perfect circle in the snow. Then, within the circle, he began quarrying out rectangular blocks. Each rectangle was about thirty inches long, twenty inches high, and eight inches wide. He cut out the rectangles quickly, curving the outer side of each just a trifle.

As he cleaved here and lopped off a bit there, the snow flew. Rawbones' fur hood disappeared in a cloud of white powder.

Soon the first tier of blocks was in place.

They formed a circle around the very hole from which they had been dug. For this tier, and for all the others to come, the blocks were interlocked. This is done so that frost will finish the job by cementing the blocks together.

Before Rawbones began the second tier, he made a diagonal cut on the top of the first one. The cut slanted inward. After that, the wall rose quickly, leaning inward—thanks to the diagonal cut on the top of the first tier—to form a dome. At the top of the dome, Rawbones inserted a keystone block. Then he chinked all the crevices with soft snow.

After that, he stood back and looked at his handiwork.

"*Ta-i-mak!*" he said proudly. "Finished!"

"Rawbones," I said, "it is a thing of beauty."

"It is nothing." He waved his knife. "I have made many better ones. Climb up on it."

"What?"

"Go ahead—right to the top!"

"And ruin all your hard work?"

Rawbones roared with laughter. "Climb up!" he ordered. "Go ahead. Climb!"

"All right!" I scrambled up the sides of the new snow house. "But don't ask me to build it over for you." At the top, I sat down gingerly, expecting the whole thing to crumble beneath me at any moment.

It didn't. I might just as well have been sitting on solid concrete.

"You see!" Rawbones shouted at me. "It is strong."

I was about to agree when a dreadful thought hit me. "But how do you get inside? There are no doors!"

"Doors! Pooh!" A few minutes later, Rawbones had carved a small square out of the lowest tier of blocks.

Later, as I would discover, he would build a tunnel leading to this small entryway. The tunnel would zigzag to discourage the dogs from coming through. Off the tunnel, Rawbones would build tiny rooms for storing food and other supplies.

"Come," he was saying. "We must go to the lake."

To the lake? I ran after him, wondering to myself, "What now?" From the surface of the lake, some hundred yards inland, Rawbones cut out a square of ice. Hurrying back to his new house, he carved another block of snow out of the wall, this time rather high up. Then he inserted the square of clear, fresh-water ice.

"Window!" he said, with a jack-o'-lantern grin.

Before I could express my admiration, he had disappeared into the snow house. I followed. Inside, toward the rear, Rawbones was building a large platform out of snow.

"Bed," he explained.

While he worked, he told me how his wife would make the bed. First she would spread on it a layer of bearskin, fur side down. Over this she would place a second layer, fur side up. Above this, more skins would be arranged to taste. The foot of the bed was toward the wall, the head toward the center of the igloo.

On either side of the entrance, Rawbones built two smaller platforms. "To hold the stone lamps," he told me.

Next he hurried out to his sled, returning with a collection of driftwood sticks. He jammed them into the wall near the lamp platforms. On these pegs, he pointed out, he and his family would hang whatever they wished to dry or thaw out: mitts, boots, frozen fish.

"There now," he grunted. "I have a winter home. Does Falla like?"

"It is a thing of beauty," I said, for perhaps the hundredth time.

"Good. I'll get my family now. We'll move in. Soon everything will be in shape. Then perhaps Falla will pay us an official visit, eh?"

"Falla," said Falla, "will be delighted."

7. ESKIMO CAMP

My official visit to Rawbones' winter home took place a few weeks later.

It was a December afternoon. Rawbones came after me with his dog sled. After a cup of scalding tea in the mission house and a brief chat, we were off.

It was the season of perpetual night. The sky above us was dazzling, dazzling beyond belief. The stars seemed to dance in their blue setting. It was as if some giant, standing on the earth, had stripped a mammoth Christmas tree of its ornaments and hurled them into the heavens. A curtainy halo rimmed the moon. The North Star glittered almost above us. The Great Bear rested on its side. The jeweled stars of Orion, the mighty hunter, seemed to be striding toward us. Through all spread the Milky Way, thick and vaporous. Occasionally, as we whipped along on Rawbones' sled, a shooting star took leave of all this brilliance and plummeted luminously down toward the horizon.

As we rounded the crest of the final hill, the Eskimo camp came into view along the shore below. Faintly bathed with the light of the star-sprinkled sky, the igloos huddled closely together. From a distance, they looked like a caravan of camels squatting in the snow to rest.

As we drew nearer, I could see the Inuit's sledges lying around. Each stood on a heaped-up snowbank, high enough to keep the dogs from reaching it and chewing up the animal-skin straps holding the sled runners together. The dogs themselves lay curled up in the snow, their feet and heads tucked snugly out of sight.

Rifles and harpoons stood at the igloo entrances, ready for use. A pale haze drifted from the domed roofs. It was a sort of reek, like the whitish smoke which comes from a chimney right after the fire has gone out. Seal-skins, drying and bleaching, waved in the icy breeze like stiffened sails.

Otherwise there was no movement, no life, no sound. For a time it was as if we were approaching a deserted village. Then the keen ears of one of the sleeping dogs picked up the crunch of our runners, and suddenly there was a pandemonium of barks and yelps.

Just as suddenly, people began crowding out of the igloos. They had to bend double, for the entryways were low and square, like the doors of a baker's oven. Even at a distance, I could hear what they were yelling.

"Travelers coming! Travelers coming! Who can they be?"

Then someone recognized our dogs. "It's Rawbones!" A chorused shout went up. "And he's bringing the Falla for a visit!"

For days, apparently, my forthcoming visit had been the talk of the village. As Rawbones braked the dogs with a ringing, "Ho! Stop!" and threw out the anchor, the villagers crowded around, shouting and laughing and loudly clapping one another on the back. Some of the faces were familiar. I had seen them off and on at the mission house. Most of the people were strangers to me.

One by one, they came up. Each touched my

hand lightly with his own by way of greeting. First the men came, then the women. The men advanced boldly, with a swagger. The women were shy. They giggled as they skittered up to me and just as rapidly skittered away. The children hung back. They clutched their mothers' parkas, their round black eyes staring with curiosity. I heard one of them mutter to his pal, "The Falla he may be, but he's a stupid Big Eyebrows all the same!"

With a wing-like wave of his arms, Rawbones cleared a path through the crowd. "Enough! Enough!" he bellowed at the others. "The Falla does not care to stand around talking, talking, talking all day, the way we do. He is tired after his journey and wishes to rest inside."

He ducked into the zigzag tunnel leading to the entryway of his house. I ducked, too. Slipping along on all fours, I bumped into a sleeping dog in the darkness. He growled and snapped at my leg. Several zigzags beyond, Rawbones dived through a second hole and I followed him. It was my first entrance into a snow house actually occupied by an Eskimo family.

A sour smell of rancid grease, wet fur, and burrow musk almost gagged me. But the big room had a bright appearance. It was pleasant and homey. The stone lamps, one on either side of the door, gave off a reddish light that spread a soft glow over the high, vault-like walls.

Rawbones' family stood waiting for us: two women, two young girls, two even younger boys.

There were introductions. The younger of the women was Rawbones' wife, On-gir-lak. She touched my hand gently with her own and bobbed her head in a sort of shy curtsy.

In their youth Eskimo women are often quite pretty. At twelve or thirteen, there is an apple bloom on their rounded cheeks. Their walk is firm and springy. But they marry early. With marriage comes hard work and endless toil. Soon their beauty passes. Although Ongirlak, Rawbones' wife, was younger than I, she already had the rough skin and faded eyes of an old woman.

The other woman was the mother of Rawbones' wife.

"Meet Granny," he said.

Granny's smile was as toothless as it was warm. Her eyes dreamed in a nest of dirt-filled wrinkles.

Obviously she was very old, for she was liberally tattooed. These days few Eskimo women are tattooed, but in the old days almost all of them were. The tattooing was executed in a painful way. The skin was pricked at thousands of points with a sharp copper needle, and the bleeding dots were smeared with soot.

The result was always the same—a hideous blue design. There were five fan-shaped markings from Granny's lower lip to the base of her chin. There were more lines from the base of her nose to the ears. Still more lines feathered out from the corners of her milky eyes. Her hands and forearms had received a similar treatment.

Like Rawbones' wife, she touched my hand and bobbed her head. "So," she said in a crackly voice, "you are the Long Robe."

"Yes," I said, "I am one of the poor parsons of the north." Everyone laughed at this, for poor parson of the north is one of the names the Inuit give us.

"I hear many things about you, Falla," the old lady went on. "I hear you want to make Christians of us all."

"Nothing would please me more. When are you coming into the fold, Granny?"

"Who, me?" She gave three dry little laughs like a series of hiccoughs. "Who would want an old husk like me?"

"God would, Granny. God loves us all."

"All?" A curious little look flickered like a candle flame in her old eyes. "All, you say? What a good, sweet God He must be!"

Meanwhile, the two girls had taken my outer garments. They shook them free of snow and folded them carefully.

Then the boys were introduced. Husky lads they were, with their plump faces and straight bobbed hair. They took one look at me and ran into a shadowy corner of the igloo, rolling over one another like playful bear cubs and giggling.

"Come out of there at once!" Ongirlak called after them.

"Oh, do be still, Ongirlak!" they yelled back.

Eskimo children always address their mother by her given name. In the Eskimo language there is no word for mother.

"Come now, Falla." With a great swing of his arms, Rawbones indicated I was to sit on the skin bed. "Be seated. And let us know, are you comfortable? Is it too hot, too cold?"

"It is a little warm," I had to admit.

"We will remedy that." Standing on the bed, Rawbones thrust a hole through the roof with his snow knife. "There, now," he cried. "Our house has a little nostril. It can breathe."

Breathe it did. I could hear the stale air hissing like steam through the newly created ventilation hole.

Rawbones hopped to the floor again and sat down beside me. "It is important," he said, "to have the temperature of the igloo exactly right. Near the freezing point is best. If it rises above that, watch out. The walls thaw and drip. At night they freeze again. Next morning, instead of a snow house, we have an icehouse. Then we have to move out and build another igloo."

He roared with laughter and shouted at his wife. "How are things going, Ongirlak? Is the meal ready? The Falla must be starved."

As a matter of fact, the Falla was not a bit hungry. But the Inuit were. They always are. They have no regular meal hours. They eat continually, at any and all hours, so long as there is anything edible around.

Already Ongirlak had trimmed the wicks in the two lamps. The water in a battered teakettle, purchased at the Coppermine trading store, burbled pleasantly above a lazy flame.

"First of all," Ongirlak announced, "let us eat our fish." She squatted on the floor. Granny and the children joined her. They formed a semicircle, with the evening meal in the center. The food rested in basins. One was filled with raw, frozen fish. In another was a pint or so of smelly seal oil.

"You first, Falla," said Ongirlak. With a greasy hand, she extracted a hunk of frozen fish, dipped it in the seal oil, and handed it to me.

There was a smile on the corners of her lips.

Looking quickly around, I could see that all of them were smiling. I knew what they were thinking. "Will the Falla," they were wondering, "accept our food, or will he shrink from it in horror the way many white men do?"

The joke was on them. I knew all about frozen fish. I had eaten it often out on the trail with one of the Inuit or another priest. I had even developed a liking for the great Eskimo delicacy, frozen fish dipped in rancid seal oil. I plopped the fish into my mouth, ate it with relish, gave my fingers a quick lick and smacked my lips.

A murmur ran around the circle—a murmur of approval.

But there were no comments. The family was seeing how good a sport I was. The test was not over yet. The Eskimos eat not only the flesh of the fish. They also eat most of the bones. Those that are too hard, they simply spit back into the serving basin from which the fish came. When I had downed my first hunk of fish, I could feel the eyes of the others fixed sternly upon me.

Again I knew what was passing through their minds. They were asking themselves, would I, or would I not, take a second helping from the basin which they had already dirtied with their half-chewed fish bones?

I did.

This time the murmur of approval was thunderous.

"Well, now, Falla!" It was Granny's quavering voice. "You eat like a real Inuk!"

"A second helping of frozen fish even, eh?" cried Rawbones, giving me an admiring—and painful—nudge with his elbow.

Our next course was half-cooked seal meat. Ongirlak brought the steaming pot from the lamp and placed it among the other basins on the floor. There followed a series of preparations. First, Ongirlak took out each piece of meat and squeezed it between her fingers to get rid of the brownish froth on it. Then she tossed into the pot a hunk of frozen caribou blood to season the caribou soup we would eat later. All this done, she tossed a hunk of meat to me and another to her husband. After this, it was every man for himself.

Rawbones consumed his meal with vigor. Taking a huge piece of meat, he stuffed it into his mouth. Then, with a quick swipe of his *oloo*, a razor-sharp knife every Eskimo carries, he snipped off the part that wouldn't go in. I kept wondering when he would bring the *oloo* too close and snip off the tip of his nose. He never did. To the best of my knowledge, no Eskimo ever has.

There were many more courses—mostly meat. Although, in recent years, the Inuit have developed a taste for the white man's flour, sugar, and other soft foods, their diet is still 90 per cent meat and fish. In the fall, the women and children search for berries. They also dig from the ground a root called *maso*. It is a tasteless dish to my way of thinking, but the Inuit like it. Their only green is a half-digested lichen and moss which they take from the stomach of the caribou. It is a deep green mush, awful to look at, but surprisingly tasty.

The meal was endless. Halfway through, I could eat no more. I had to give up. Rawbones laughed at me. "It is true then," he cried. "You Big Eyebrows have a watch in your stomach."

The others roared at his joke, but there was no annoyance in their eyes. They liked me. I had passed the big tests. I had eaten frozen fish with rancid oil; I had taken a second helping out of the dirty basin.

When, at long last, the meal was ended, Rawbones jumped to his feet. He stretched himself and waved his short arms.

"All right, girls," he shouted to his daughters, "call in the neighbors. We will tell stories and sing songs. We will show the Falla what a good time we Inuit can have!"

8. A SWEET OLD CANNIBAL

In a matter of minutes the igloo was full of people. Soon every member of the village was on hand. They crowded the big room. Its vaulted ceiling echoed with their laughter and talk.

Never before had I seen so many Eskimos at such close range. I found myself studying them closely. Every one was clad in skins—muffled in them from head to foot. Every man carried a long knife tucked into his belt. Every one, the women as well as the men, wore a caribou parka, bearskin pants and sealskin boots. A few of the men, not many, had beards.

Eskimos have broad flat features and high cheek bones. Their heads narrow toward the top. Their cheeks are plump. Their mouths split wide open over a dropping lower lip. Their noses are short and snubby, almost without a bridge. Their eyes are small, black and brilliant, dancing in their sharply defined sockets. Their complexion is dull brown or dusky yellow, somewhat like dulled copper.

In their heavy skins, they look awkward—but they aren't. They are fine athletes and graceful dancers. They are good actors, too, and wonderful mimics. "Meet Falla," Rawbones cried, introducing me to a young Eskimo hunter.

"But I have already met him!" The youth had to shout to be heard above the surrounding hubbub. "I have heard him preach at the mission house."

Then and there he leaped onto the bed and gave an imitation of the Falla preaching. He spewed out a stream of words. The words were meaningless, but he delivered them in a perfect imitation of my voice and manner. I had to laugh. Everybody laughed.

Then there was singing.

Many of the songs were what the Inuit call laments. A man leaped onto the bed. He was a slender Eskimo with such broad shoulders that even in his thick skins he had the shape of a stubby T.

"The song I am about to sing," he announced, "is very sad. The words are those of a man who is dead. He is lying in his grave, and, of course, he wishes he were still among the living."

Thereupon the young Eskimo launched into the most mournful verse I had ever heard. Soon all the others were singing with him. In a strange minor key they sang, their voices high and wailing:

"Say, tell me now, was life so nice on earth?
There I was full of joy every time the dawn
came upon the sky
And the sun glided across the sky.
But now I lie in fright and quivering
With maggots and with crawling lice. . . .
Hi, ya a a a ya!
Hi, ya a a a ya!"

Next came dancing. From a dark corner, Rawbones brought out the drum. It was about two feet in diameter and made of the white skin of a caribou, stretched taut on a wooden ring. With a short stick, he beat on the drum. As he started to do so, the others pushed back against the wall, jamming tightly together to leave an open space in the center.

Boom! Boom!

Twirling the drum very slowly at first, then somewhat faster, Rawbones struck it at each turn. Harder and harder he struck it, gradually increasing his tempo. In no time at all, the rhythm became contagious. One Eskimo, then another, then another began to sway.

Suddenly, another man was out in the open space dancing, his knees bending, his shoulders twisting. He leaped into the air, turning as he did so with a hard and broken movement.

Boom! Boom! Boom!

The drumbeats were coming faster now, louder and more insistent. The new dancer in the center launched into wild contortions. Savage yells burst from his mouth.

Hi ya aa aa aa ya!

Soon everybody was swaying and twisting with him. Soon everybody was yelling:

Hi ya aa aa aa ya!
Hi ya aa aa aa ya!

After the dancing the storytelling began. Swapping yarns is one of the Eskimos' greatest pleasures. In those days, I did not know the Eskimo language as I know it now. I could follow an ordinary conversation, but I could not always follow the Inuit's long and involved stories of daring deeds on the sea ice and of great battles with Nanuk, the giant polar bear.

Unable to understand the stories, I sat back against the wall and carried on a conversation in low tones with Granny.

"How is it," I asked the old woman, "that you never come to the mission house? Rawbones comes from time to time to listen to my instructions. But I never see you there."

Granny's wrinkles ran together as she laughed. "Now, now, Falla," she chided, "you must not try to make a Christian of me."

"Why not?"

"Because I am too wicked. I am a very wicked old woman."

"I don't believe it, Granny. What terrible things have you done?"

For a second Granny looked away as though trying to reach back into a dim and misted past. "Once, Falla," she said, turning back to me, "I was a cannibal."

I was startled. Ordinarily Eskimos do not eat human flesh. I had heard, however, that in the old days when the hunting got bad they sometimes did.

"Tell me about it, Granny," I said.

"Well, Falla, it was a long time ago. Times were very bad. We could not kill a thing."

"Were there no seals around?" I asked. "No caribou?"

"Oh, yes, plenty of seals. Plenty of caribou, too. But some Inuit living to the east of us had thrown a curse on us. We could no longer kill game."

"And what happened?" I asked.

"We starved," she said simply. "Soon we began eating the fallen ones. The old people died first and quickly. Then some of the others. Before long, there were only a few of us left."

I looked at her ancient face and my heart was filled with pity. Again Granny turned her eyes away for a moment. Then, "The last time I ate human flesh," she said, "it was my little brother that I ate. I had loved him. He was always kind to me."

"Don't think of it, Granny," I urged her. "It is all so long ago."

I was about to question the sweet old cannibal further, but just then a roar of laughter rolled through the room. Someone had finished a rattling good story.

On the heels of the laughter, Rawbones sprang to his feet. "Enough for one evening," he shouted. "Surely the Falla will be wanting some sleep now."

As if dispersed by gunshot, the visitors fell to their knees and dived into the night. It was astonishing how quickly they disappeared.

I was tired, too tired to pay much attention to the many going-to-bed procedures. The last thing I remember is seeing Ongirlak, Rawbones' wife, lower the light in the stone lamps. She did this by patting the fire down with her hands. Soon nothing remained but a wavering sliver of flame in the corners of the two lamps. Then Ongirlak shoved a block of snow into the entryway, closing it for the night.

After which we slept, each in his fur sleeping bag.

9. A DAY IN THE IGLOO

Granny and the children shook me awake the next morning. Ongirlak was already up and busy. She leaned over the lamps, straightening the wicks and blowing up the flames.

In a few minutes the igloo was brightly lighted. Last night the walls had been gray blue. This morning they were totally white, covered with a fine frost. I turned in my fur bed and a shower of ice particles, shaken off the walls by the movement, completed my awakening.

Rawbones slept on, but not for long. Soon the tantalizing smell of brewing tea brought his eyes open. As I crawled from my sleeping bag and started dressing, he looked at me with surprise. He said nothing, but I could read his thoughts.

"Only a stupid Big Eyebrows," he was telling himself, "would get up with the women. As for me, I shall lie here and let them serve me."

Serve him they did. He received his breakfast in bed—a mug of tea and a slab of frozen fish. Then he lay there another half hour, describing in a rambling way the dreams he had had during the night.

"The weather is nice," Ongirlak said after a while. "Not too cold. Not a breath of wind, either."

His wife's remark brought Rawbones to life. "My boots!" he commanded, leaping from the bed. His brow was furrowed with thought. What should he do today? Look to his traps? Seek for caribou? Hunt seals? Finally he decided.

"I shall go to the river and come back tonight. With fish, eh?"

Dressed at last, he grabbed an empty basin and went outside. I crawled after him through the entryway tunnel. As Ongirlak had said, the day was windless and pleasant. A pale glow lay along the horizon and bright stars dotted the sky.

From under the snow, Rawbones dug a large hunk of tundra and placed it in the basin.

"Let me," I said, taking the basin from him.

"You know how to do it, Falla?"

"Of course," I said. "I've done it many times."

Back in the igloo, I placed the basin over one of the stone lamps. As the dirt inside melted, I stirred it until I had a gooey mess. When the mess reached the consistency of bread dough, I carried it outside. There Rawbones packed his sled runners with the melted dirt. We stood and chatted while the dirt froze hard. Then Rawbones planed it down with his knife so that his sled would run level.

Next I brought him a basin of water and a bearskin rag. He took some of the water in his mouth. Spitting on the rag from time to time, he rubbed the runners vigorously. The water froze on the packed mud at once, forming a high, slick glaze.

These operations are known as packing the runners and icing them. As a rule, the runners of the long, low Eskimo sledge are made of wood or whalebone. Some Eskimos use the steel runners on sale at the trading posts. Most do not. They have found that in bitter cold the metal tends to stick to ice and snow. Whatever the material of the runners, they must be repacked with dirt every few days. On the trail, the packing must be iced every three hours.

His sled ready, Rawbones got his harpoon and rifle. His wife harnessed the dogs. Rawbones seated himself on the sled, pulled up the anchor, and growled an order. The dogs, full of ginger after their night's rest, made a bolt for it, bouncing the sled from snowbank to snowbank. Some 500 yards away, the lead dog stumbled. The others piled up against him. Sled and driver twisted over in a whirling pinwheel of snow, and the morning air crackled with Rawbones' choicest cursing.

Standing beside me at the igloo entrance, Ongirlak chuckled. "But there," I heard her mutter to herself, "I can't be standing here all day watching my silly husband tumbling in the snow. There is work to be done."

And what work! All day Ongirlak kept at it. Even when a neighbor woman dropped in during the afternoon for a mug of tea and a chat, Ongirlak went right on working.

First she folded the bedding and strewed the igloo floor with fresh clean snow. Then, seating herself tailor-fashion near one of the lamps, she took up her sewing and mending. She examined the family garments one by one. She stretched and softened the tough skin with her teeth. She made a patch here. She closed up a rent seam there.

Watching her, I marveled for the hundredth time at the beauty and workmanship of Eskimo clothes. No better clothes for cold weather are made anywhere in the world.

Except for slight differences in the cut and length of the parka, Eskimo clothing is the same everywhere. The same materials are used. Caribou is the basic fur, preferably the skin of caribou killed in the early fall. Before becoming a garment, the skin is dried in the sun for a few days. Then it is scraped clean and softened with sharp iron or bone tools. Sometimes the trousers are made of seal or bearskin. Bearskin is very warm. It never gets wet and it lasts for years. Boots are made of sealskin. All of the Eskimos' winter garments are light, windproof, and dry. They are soft as velvet and extraordinarily comfortable.

On the trail in bitter weather, the Eskimo wears a double layer of skins. Warm air circulating between the two layers insulates him against the chill winds. The undergarments—shirt, drawers and socks—are usually made of the skin of a fawn, with the fur side turned inward against the body. The heavier outer garments—

trousers and coat—are made with the fur side out. Like all Eskimo clothing, the coat is without buttons. It slips over the head. The Eskimo name for it is *koo-li-tak*. We know it as the parka, from the Russian word for blouse.

All the work that goes into making these fine clothes is done by the Eskimo housewife. She scrapes and tans the skins. She sews the garments. For thread she uses the long, flat sinew of the caribou backbone. She molds the boot soles to fit. Her tool for this is her own teeth. She bites innumerable folds into the skin until it resembles the elbow of a stovepipe. She does this by the hour. By the time the Eskimo woman is thirty or so, her teeth are worn down to almost nothing.

All day, during my visit to Rawbones' igloo, his wife, Ongirlak, mended and sewed and scraped and tanned. She paused only to feed the children, trim the lamp wicks, and make tea for me.

As for me, I spent much of the day outside watching the children at their play. The little girls played house with some ugly dolls their mother had made for them out of scraps of fur and bits of driftwood. They housed their dolls in tiny igloos which they built by the dozen in the snow. The boys raced up and down snowbanks on their miniature sleds. They shot at nothing with their miniature bows and arrows.

The night before, the children had been shy with me. After I had been around for a while in the morning, they got used to me.

The smallest boy, a handsome, black-eyed lad, even brought a piece of knotted string and showed me how he could shape it into various designs. Twisting the string between his stubby fingers, he made the design of a seal. Later he made one which he said was a caribou. I couldn't see the caribou myself, but I willingly took his word for it.

"How many designs can you make with your string?" I asked him.

"Man," was his prompt reply.

For a second, I was puzzled. Then it came to me. The Inuit count on their fingers and toes. A man has ten fingers and ten toes. Therefore "man" equals twenty. Rawbones' youngest son could make "man"—that is, twenty—designs.

During the afternoon, the boy startled me by climbing to the top of the igloo, dragging his sled after him. Then, with a great shout, he took a whirlwind slide down the steep sides. The crunch of his sled runners could be heard inside the snow house. I expected to see his mother at once. I expected to see her come running out of the house, protesting loudly.

I should have known better. Eskimo parents, as I was to see more fully later, never scold their children. They seldom tell them what to do or not to do. They let them do pretty much as they please. In short, they spoil them.

The reason for this goes back to an ancient Eskimo custom. When an Eskimo man grows old, he can no longer hunt and fish. When a woman grows old, she can no longer mend and sew and scrape and tan. In the harsh, cold country of Eskimoland, such old people are looked upon as useless. They are merely mouths to feed. This raises a problem in a country where food is difficult and dangerous to get.

In the old days, young Eskimos solved this problem by putting their aging parents to death. As a rule, they simply put them in a deserted igloo and left them there to starve. I wish I could say that this happened *only* in the past. I am sorry to say that, once in a great while, it happens even now.

It explains why Eskimo parents rarely scold or speak harshly to their children. They desperately want their children's good will and approval. After all, the children will grow up soon. Then it will be they—the children—who will decide whether the old people in the family are put to death or are permitted to live out their days.

Toward evening, Rawbones' boys and girls

wearied of playing and we all drifted into the brightly lighted igloo. Sitting down in a corner, I had another little talk with Granny.

Granny, of course, was one of the useless old Eskimos. She had done nothing all day. She had merely sat near one of the stone lamps, sometimes sleeping, sometimes humming an ancient Eskimo ballad. She was like an old clock that has run down.

"Granny," I said to her, "have you any idea how old you are?"

"No idea at all," she replied. "I only know that I am too old. My daughter loves me and permits me to live. It is kind of her, but sometimes I think it would be better if she and Rawbones simply took me out on the sea ice and left me there. Then I would not be in the way and . . ."

Granny left off suddenly and gave me an embarrassed look.

"But I should not say these things to you, Falla!" she said. "I hear you Christians do not believe in killing any one."

"That is correct, Granny. We believe that creatures to whom God has given a soul and whom He has put on this earth, only God has the right to take away."

Granny shot me a searching look. "Tell me more about your beliefs, Falla."

I did so gladly. To my surprise, the old woman stayed awake and listened. I talked for almost an hour. I told her the story of our Lord. I told her how He had died for our sins. I told her about the rules He left to guide us in this world so that we might share the next with Him. I went on talking until I saw that Granny was on the verge of dozing off.

When I stopped, she nodded her old head a few times. "I like what you have told me, Falla," she said. "Yes, I can see that your Church, the Church of the Long Robes, is a kind, bright Church."

She mumbled something more—something that I was unable to catch—and fell asleep.

At that moment I had the strong and happy feeling that Granny would die a Christian. I can tell you now that a few months later she did.

10. ROUGH CHARACTERS AND WEDDING BELLS

Among my good friends at Coppermine was a young Eskimo called Tu-lu-gak. We had often hunted together. We had faced many dangers together. One winter word reached us that Tulugak's family—his parents and his brothers and sisters—were starving in an Eskimo camp many miles inland from the Arctic Ocean. Together we went after them with our sleds and brought them to the shore where game was plentiful.

A few days later, Tulugak came smiling into the mission house. He brought great news. He was about to marry.

"And who," I asked him, "is the lucky girl?"

"She is one of yours, Falla."

"A Christian?"

"Yes, Falla. The one you call Bessie."

"I'm delighted for you, Tulugak." I gave him my hand in congratulation. Tulugak grinned and went on his way, humming an Eskimo tune. "There goes a contented man," I remember saying to myself. "He hasn't a worry in the world."

That evening I learned that Tulugak had many worries. It was right after the supper hour. The other young priest and I had just finished our meal by the coal stove. We had started to wash the dishes when a loud and agitated knocking rattled the mission house door.

Before I could reach it, the door opened.

For a second, the misty winter night framed the figure of a pretty Eskimo girl. Then the door was closed and she was inside, leaning against the door and breathing hard.

Her clothes were torn, her hair disarrayed. Her eyes were filled with terror. At first I didn't recognize her. Then, "Why, it's Bessie!" I heard my priest companion saying.

"Why, so it is." I hurried to the terrified girl. "What is it, Bessie? What's the matter?"

"It's Tulugak, Falla."

"Tulugak?"

"He wants to marry me."

"Wants to? I thought it was all set."

"It is all set. My father arranged it. But only just now, out there . . ." The girl made a wild gesture in the direction of the mission house window. "Only just now out there," she repeated, "I met Tulugak. I told him I didn't want to marry him. I'm a Christian, I told him. A Christian girl can marry whom she pleases."

The girl burst into tears. "Oh, Falla, I have never seen Tulugak so angry. He got a crazy look in his eyes. He chased me. I'm afraid he's going to kill me!"

"Now, now, Bessie," I said, "stop your crying." I led her to one of the benches and made her sit down. "Calm yourself now. No harm can come to you here."

I would have spoken further, but just then there was a loud stomping and grunting outside the mission door. The other priest and I exchanged glances.

"I think," he said, "that we're going to have company."

"Yes." I nodded. "And I think our company is Tulugak."

It was. He threw open the door and banged in. It was a Tulugak I'd never seen before. His face was working in an ugly manner. His dark eyes were blazing. Before I could stop him, he had rushed across the room to Bessie. He grabbed her by the hair. He was dragging her toward the door when I stepped between them. I brought my hand down hard on his forearm, forcing him to release her.

"Now look, Tulugak," I said, "you can't act the rough character in here. This girl is under my protection. You leave her alone."

"But she's my wife, Falla—or will be soon!"

"If she wishes to be," I yelled at him.

"What have her wishes to do with it?" Tulugak gave me a scornful look. "She's a woman. A woman is nothing. A woman is less than a dog, and like a dog she does what she is told!"

He made for Bessie again, but with a shove I sent him spinning to the floor. He shook himself, got to his feet and faced me.

I examined him carefully. He was without weapons, I saw—no knife at his belt, no rifle in his hand. Apparently Tulugak sensed what was going through my mind. He stole a quick look at the still open mission house door. I grasped the meaning of his look at once. His rifle was out there. Entering his igloo, an Eskimo always plants his rifle by the entryway. On entering the mission house, Tulugak had done so from force of habit.

I spoke quickly to the other priest in French. "His rifle's at the front door. Slip out the back way and get it."

Tulugak's puzzled gaze followed the other priest as he left the room. His eyes shot fire as he snarled at me, "A fight then, eh?"

"If it's to be a fight," I said, "I'm game."

At those words, as I had expected, Tulugak moved quickly to the front door. But he was too late. Even as he went out, the young priest came in from the rear storeroom. "It's all right," he told me in French. "The rifle is where he can't get at it."

Tulugak had returned. "My rifle!" he demanded.

"If it's to be a fight," I repeated, "let's get it over with."

It was a fight all right. Tulugak didn't lack strength or courage, but I had the advantage of height and weight. Besides, Tulugak knew nothing about boxing, and I did. A few solid rights, and it was all over. Then I picked up Tulugak and tossed him out into the snow like a sack of meal. We could hear him stomping away into the night, cursing as only an Eskimo can curse.

I turned to the girl. "All right now, Bessie," I said, "tell me all about it."

She did, brokenly, stopping now and then for another round of tears. It was the old, sad story. Among Eskimos, as Tulugak had said, a woman is nothing. She is less than nothing. The man is the boss, and the woman does as he commands.

She is lucky if she is allowed to live at all. The Eskimos kill their newborn babies frequently and for a variety of reasons.

A baby born in the summer is often quickly done away with. At this time, the family is usually on the trail, wandering from place to place. There is no time to bother with an infant, so the newborn child is simply taken out onto the steppes and stoned to death.

The problem of twins is handled in the same way. For the first three years of his life, an Eskimo baby lives on his mother's back, snug inside her parka. Alas, there is room for only one child in the parka. When twins come along, one of them is quickly disposed of.

This terrible custom is hardest of all on girl babies. A girl cannot grow up to be a hunter or fisherman. Only a certain number of them are needed to mend and sew and tan and scrape. So many girl babies are slain immediately after birth.

If a girl is permitted to live, she faces a life that is little better than that of a slave. At thirteen or fourteen, she marries—or, rather, is married. As a rule, her father and her future husband arrange the marriage between them. Her wishes are not consulted, unless . . .

Unless, like Bessie, she has become a convert to Christianity. Then she sometimes is permitted to choose her own husband. I say "sometimes" because, while Christianity has brought some freedom to the Eskimo women, it has, as yet, by no means freed them entirely. The Inuit accept new customs slowly. Their old ones die hard, very hard indeed.

All this and more Bessie and I discussed in the mission house that night. "So, Bessie," I said at length, "you are definitely against marrying Tulugak?"

"Yes, Falla. I do not like that bad-tempered man."

"Could it be," I asked gently, "that you have another preference?"

For the first time all evening, Bessie's eyes brightened. She smiled. "Yes, Falla, I have." She named a young Eskimo convert. "And he wants to marry me, too," she added.

"Has he asked you?"

"No, Falla."

"Then how do you know he wants you?"

Bessie dropped her eyes. She became all blushes and smiles. "I just know, Falla," she said. "A girl always knows when a man likes her."

"Very well." I got to my feet. "Perhaps we can do something about it. Go and bring your father to me."

In half an hour she was back, bringing the old man. He was a hard-faced, stolid Eskimo, but I knew that, like his daughter, he was a staunch convert. Carefully and gently I explained the Christian attitude toward love and marriage.

"You see," I told the old man, "just as God wants us to love Him, not because we have to but because we want to, so a woman should marry, not because she has to but because she wants to. Freedom of choice, we call it; and to us, freedom of choice is an essential part of the sacrament of marriage."

The old man listened hard. I repeated everything I had said for the second time.

The old man scratched his head. "You mean, Falla, the woman can decide?"

"Of course!"

"Ridiculous!" The old man snorted. "Why should you Long Robes worry about women? Aren't you men yourselves?"

"Women are people," I told him. "They have souls, just as men do."

"True, Falla, but . . ."

"That's the way it is," I put in, "and that's the way it's going to be."

The old man shrugged. "All right, Falla," he grunted, "you are the doctor. Of course I will do as you say. But please don't tell people I had any part in it. It is against our customs. The other Inuit will not approve."

I was on my feet before he had finished. "Good!" I said. "Bessie, go get your young man—the one you like."

I had decided that it would be best to act fast. If I delayed, there might be trouble. Tulugak and his friends might kick up a row. Tulugak might even seize Bessie and force her to go away with him. Such things happen among the Inuit.

Bessie wasted no time in bringing her young man to the mission house. He, in turn, brought his whole family. Before midnight that very evening, Bessie and her true love were man and wife.

Of course, there was still Tulugak to be dealt with. There was nothing he could do about Bessie now, but I still had his gun. I figured he would do something about that.

He did. Early the next morning a member of his family, a small boy, came around to the mission house.

"Tulugak sent me for his rifle," he said.

"If Tulugak wants his rifle," I told him, "he will have to come for it himself. Tell him that, will you?"

Tulugak did come, very quiet now, his anger gone. He held his head high. "I have come for my rifle," he said.

"Do you still want to kill me?"

He didn't answer.

"Say it!" I commanded. "Speak! Do you want to kill me?"

"No, Falla."

"All right," I said. I was holding his rifle in my hands, the muzzle pointed directly at him. The night before, the other priest and I had examined it. We had found a cartridge in the chamber and six more in the magazine—quite enough to do away with me. When, after a moment, I turned the gun around and handed it to Tulugak, everything was the same. There was still a shell in the chamber.

Tulugak and I stood facing each other. The tables were now turned. The gun was pointing directly at me, and I couldn't help but wonder —would Tulugak keep his word or would he kill me on the spot? A second passed, two seconds. . . . Then, abruptly, Tulugak turned and strode out of the mission house.

But he was back that afternoon, all smiles.

"Suppose we hunt a few seals together, eh, Falla?" he cried, and we were off. We were friends again. When I asked him, just for fun, what he thought of Bessie's marriage, he merely shrugged.

"*Pirtok!*" he said. "Nothing—one can do nothing about it!"

11. JOURNEY TO THE END OF THE WORLD

North of the mainland of Canada is a large island called Victoria. Many Copper Eskimos live along the southern and western shores of Victoria. They live at places called Cambridge Bay, Prince Albert Sound, Minto, and Walker Bay. Their most northerly settlements are at Pemmican Point, far up in the northwest corner of the island.

The Copper Eskimos of Victoria are spoken of as the last people on earth. North of their camps and igloos nobody lives, nobody at all. Between Pemmican Point and the North Pole, there is nothing, nothing but uninhabited islands and the vast Arctic Sea.

At Coppermine, during the long winter evenings, we priests often talked about Victoria Island.

"How wonderful it would be," I remember one of the priests saying one evening, "to set up a mission on Victoria Island."

The rest of us nodded. Each of us was thinking the same thing. Each was hoping that he would be the priest chosen to set up a mission at Victoria, a mission to the last people on earth.

Early in 1937, my third year at Coppermine, a letter arrived from my superior, Bishop Breynat, of Fort Smith, Canada. The letter was addressed to me. I read it—not once—but many times. I could hardly believe my eyes.

I had been chosen to go to Victoria!

"Mind you," Bishop Breynat wrote, "I am not saying that we will definitely establish a mission there. First, I wish you to explore the island. Make a sketch map of it. Find out how many Eskimos live there."

Explore the island! Make maps! Take a census of the people! When I reached this part of Bishop Breynat's letter, I grew so excited I had to put it down for a few minutes. Finally, I picked it up and read on.

"After you have finished your explorations," the bishop wrote, "return to Coppermine. I will join you there at Eastertime. We will talk things over. If your report indicates that a mission on Victoria would do some good, I will then authorize you to set one up."

The bishop had given me four weeks. Four weeks in which to travel over 800 miles. With nine good dogs out in front, a sixteen-foot Eskimo sled can carry 1,000 pounds at a fast clip. I loaded mine to the limit. After all, Eskimoland isn't Boston. There are no hotels along the trail, no restaurants, no stores. It is often 200 or 300 miles between camps.

On the sled went fur bedding and spare clothing, provisions, a kerosene lamp, kerosene stove and fuel, cooking utensils, tools, rope, medicine, matches, and tobacco. On it, too, went an extra snow knife. If you break your only snow knife on the trail, you're out of luck. You can't build any more igloos, and, without shelter, the Arctic traveler is done for.

I had two companions. One of them was an Eskimo guide, a broad-shouldered young fellow whom we addressed simply as Boy. The other was Frenchy Chartrand of the Royal Canadian Mounted Police.

I was pleased as punch when young Frenchy offered to go along.

"But why do you wish to visit Victoria Island?" I asked him. "Are there criminals among the Eskimos there?"

"Criminals among the Eskimos?" Frenchy exclaimed. "Whoever heard of such a thing?"

We both laughed, for, of course, Frenchy was joking. Crime is common among the Eskimos.

Except for those who have become Christians, the Eskimos have almost no religion. Their songs and stories tell us that long ago they had one, but over the centuries it has disappeared.

Today they have only a few superstitions, which they do not take very seriously. Their moral code is simple. Rawbones explained it to me one morning.

"We do not care what a man does," he said, "so long as his actions do not hinder the hunting and fishing on which our lives depend."

So Inuk does as he pleases. He murders, he steals, he lies; and the other Inuit think no less of him for it. When I first came to the Arctic, fresh out of the seminary, I was shocked by these things. After a while, I got used to them. I learned to remind myself of the Lord's words on the cross:

Father, forgive them, for they know not what they do.

A fine snow was in the air as we took off for Victoria, our two sleds groaning with supplies. We headed almost due north across the ice of Coronation Gulf.

For miles we had to carve out a trail with axes. Again, and again, ragged hummocks of snow overturned the sleds, sending our supplies flying in all directions. The dogs grew tired and became unruly. We ran along beside them to keep them in order. Soon we were soaking with sweat. The moment we stopped to rest, our clothes froze to our skins.

We spent our first night on the open ice. We should have built an igloo, but, frankly, we were too tired. "After all," said Boy, our young Eskimo guide, "the snow is high here. We can dig a cave for the night." We did. We scooped out a sizable one in the snow on the side away from the wind. We ate a quick meal of tea and frozen fish. We squirmed into our fur-lined bags and slept. How we slept!

The next morning the trail was still bad. Toward noon a sound like the twanging of distant wires reached our ears. Frenchy Chartrand grabbed my arm, bringing me to a halt. A scowl darkened his strong features. "Father!"

He leaned forward a little, peering in the direction of the sound. "I believe we are in for a powder mill."

A powder mill! Frenchy had spoken the most terrible words in the northland. "Powder mill" (*le poudrerie* in French) is the old French-Canadian woodsman's name for the Arctic blizzard.

It was upon us almost at once. We had just time to dig another cave and scramble into it. A second later the world around us went mad as a howling, smashing wind tore and gouged at the snow, choking the air with a fine, stinging powder.

"Where are the winds coming from?" I yelled at Frenchy above the turmoil.

His answer was a shouted "Who knows?"

Indeed, the winds seemed to be coming in all directions. Boy, the Eskimo guide, shrank into his corner and grinned. "*Pirtok!*" he shrugged. "Nothing—one can do nothing about it."

He was right. We could only crouch inside our snow cavern and wait. Only a fool tries to travel in an Arctic blizzard. Northland hunters have been known to leave their cabins and venture into its raging winds, only to die a few feet from their front doors.

It lasted about an hour. Then it was gone.

A sudden silence succeeded it, an eerie calm. During the rest of the day, we made good time, for the blizzard winds had rearranged the landscape. They had leveled the snow somewhat, giving us a faster trail.

Dusk brought us to the first Eskimo settlement, a cluster of igloos on Read Island, a few miles below the southwest shore of Victoria. The barking of the dogs announced our arrival and brought the Eskimos streaming out of their igloos on all fours. Twilight had set in. The Inuit gathered close in an effort to make out our faces.

The sight of Boy delighted them. They thumped their fellow-Eskimo on the back and shouted welcoming words to him. With Frenchy and myself, they kept their distance.

Seeing this, Frenchy lifted his hand for silence. He introduced himself as a member of the Royal Canadian Mounted Police. Then he introduced me, saying, "And I have brought the Falla with me."

He had no sooner finished speaking than the villagers scattered in all directions. In what seemed no time at all, they were back in their igloos. The three of us—Boy, Frenchy and I—stood alone in what suddenly seemed a town without inhabitants.

I looked at Frenchy and he at me.

"One thing is obvious," he said. "Either these Inuit don't like police, or they don't like priests."

"Or both!" I suggested.

"Well," chuckled Frenchy, "I guess we throw up our own igloo tonight."

"We will do nothing of the sort," I told him. "I'm here to talk to these people, and talk to them I shall." I cast my eyes around. Near by was a very large igloo, a fancy one with a porch. "We will spend the night there," I said, pointing to it.

I spoke with confidence. Whatever their defects, the Inuit have one greatly endearing virtue. They are hospitable to a fault. Whoever enters an Eskimo home receives food and bed for the night. To share with a stranger is an unwritten law among the people of the north, one that is rarely broken.

I headed for the big igloo, Frenchy and Boy behind me. Frenchy was laughing to himself. "Lead on, Father," he was saying. "I've been kicked out of better snow houses than this."

"We will not be kicked out," I told him.

It was 40° below zero outside, and, in the beginning, the welcome we received within was only one degree warmer. But welcomed we were. The woman of the family brought us basins of frozen fish and bear meat. We were even offered that prize Eskimo potion, a drink of blood from a caribou killed that afternoon.

Nor did we eat in silence. I talked. I put questions to the Eskimos. How many people were living in this village? How many were living farther north along the shores of Victoria Island? Were there any Catholic converts among them? Could they give me any idea of a good site on which to set up a mission for Victoria?

There were no answers to my questions, but shortly the Eskimos began muttering to themselves. As I was talking myself, I didn't catch their words, but Frenchy did. "They are saying, Father," he told me, "that you talk Eskimo better than any white man they have ever heard. They think it is most courteous of you to have gone to the trouble of learning their difficult language. In short, they are beginning to think well of you."

A few minutes later we were all good pals. The head of the family excused himself. He was out of the igloo only a few minutes. When he returned, the entire village was at his heels.

There was a noisy ceremony of greeting during which everyone touched our hands—mine, Frenchy's and Boy's. The men first, boldly; then the women, shyly. I put my questions again. This time they were answered. The Eskimos asked me questions. They wanted to know all about the beliefs of the Church, all about our Lord and His Blessed Mother.

For an hour or more, I talked of these wondrous things. Then, remembering the Eskimos' love of mimicry, I stood up and gave them an imitation of their actions when Frenchy and Boy and I had first arrived in their village. My efforts brought a roar of laughter that a Broadway actor would have envied.

After that, we capped off a pleasant evening with songs and storytelling.

It was about the same at all of the camps on Victoria Island. At first, the Eskimos were standoffish, sometimes hostile. Sooner or later, except for the inhabitants of one small settlement, they came around.

On March 19, 1937, we were at a camp on the north side of the mouth of Prince Albert Sound. There were still more camps to the north, but my time was up. In fact, to reach Coppermine by Easter, we would have to cover, in eight days, a distance that had taken us sixteen days coming up.

Fortunately, the trail going back was not bad. There was only one serious mishap. One evening, stopping for the night at an abandoned igloo, I noticed that the mud packing on my sledge runners was almost gone. I gazed about at the snow. It would be a long, hard job digging through for a hunk of dirt.

Boy came up with an idea. "The oatmeal, Falla," he said. "Cook up some of your oatmeal, and put that on the runners. It is as good as mud."

No sooner said than done. I then slipped into the igloo for a welcome snooze. Two hours later, I ventured out to see if my oatmeal packing had frozen solid enough to be planed down. When I reached the sled, I got a lesson in what makes the Eskimos swear so outrageously.

My sled runners were bare!

Looking around, I quickly saw the reason why. My nine dogs were licking their chops. In fact, I could have sworn that those fuzzy rascals were grinning at me. They had eaten my oatmeal packing, every swollen grain of it.

12. MASS IN THE SHADOW OF THE NORTH POLE

My report on Victoria Island, handed to Bishop Breynat at Coppermine on Easter of 1937, was satisfactory. After five months of thought and planning, His Lordship ordered me to return to Victoria and set up a mission. To say that I was pleased is to put it mildly. To think that I, the humblest of men, had been selected to plant the cross farther north than it had ever been carried!

My mission—the Mission of Christ the King

—was a simple, frame structure in the little trading village of King's Bay at the mouth of Prince Albert Sound on Victoria Island.

During most of the early years on the island, however, I headquartered at Minto, another tiny village some miles to the north. I say "headquartered," because a missionary to a wandering people like the Eskimos must be a wanderer himself. Sometimes I spent three fourths of the year on the trail, traveling from camp to camp up and down the shores of Victoria.

But when I was home in those beginning years, home was the shack at Minto. I built a chapel in one corner. The altar was constructed of packing boxes topped with a tabernacle made of an empty ammunition case.

It was not the most elegant of churches, but to me, it was beautiful. As for our Lord, I need not tell you that He Who was born in a manger did not shun to dwell in my simple house.

I had one assistant, a young Eskimo convert named Tom Goose. Tom was a robust, sparkling-eyed fellow, full of fun. We had known each other at Coppermine where, for some years, Tom had done odd jobs for the Royal Canadian Mounted Police. When, shortly before leaving Coppermine, I heard that Tom had left his job, I got in touch with him in a hurry.

"Look here, Tom," I said, "I'll need a helper up on Victoria Island. How about coming along with me?"

"And bring my wife?"

"Of course bring your wife."

We traveled north together. The trip was without adventure, except for an incident that might have been serious. One stormy evening, in darkness, we pulled up for the night. As I hopped off my sled, I happened to glance at Tom's sled—and did a double-take.

"Excuse me, Tom," I called to him. "I was under the impression that you were married."

Tom grinned and said, "Oh, yes, Falla."

"Well, then, what have you done with your wife?"

"What? My wife? But there she is." He gestured toward his sled, took a look in the direction of his gesture, and screamed. "*Ma-mi-a-nar! Ma-mi-a-nar!* Calamity! Calamity! I have lost my wife!"

We doubled back on the trail and found her shortly. She was stumbling along in the darkness, crying, tired, and more frightened than hurt. In the darkness, urging his dogs forward against a furious snowfall, Tom had not noticed that his wife had fallen off the sled.

Shortly after we had settled on Victoria, I set out on my first missionary journey. I headed north. Five days later I reached Pemmican Point. I found only one Eskimo family there. During the evening they listened to me for a long while in silence.

Finally, "What do you think about becoming Christians?" I asked them.

The man of the family got to his feet. He made a long speech. Boiled down, it went something like this:

"Yes. From other Eskimos we have heard of the white man's God. But never yet has a man of prayer come to us. Aren't you the first one?"

Eskimo-fashion, he answered his own question. "Yes, you are. So we will follow you."

There was a long, solemn silence in the igloo. Then something prompted me to ask, "Are there more families to the north of us here? More Eskimos?"

"No, Falla, we are the last."

This was the moment I had waited for. His words, it seemed to me, were the words I had waited to hear all my life. These people—this squat, broad-faced man in his skins, his wife, his fur-clad children—they were, in truth, the last people on earth. And soon they would be Catholics!

"Glory to Christ the King!" I spoke aloud. Running through my mind were the words of the Gradual for the Mass for the first day of the year: "No corner of the world but has witnessed how our God can save."

There were other conversions, but they came slowly, very slowly. In those early years on Victoria, I often said Mass alone.

I remember a certain winter day in my little shack at Minto. It happened to be an Oblate feast day—the one hundred and twenty-second anniversary of the founding of my order.

In honor of the occasion, I lighted two new candles. I donned my nicest—in fact, my only—altar vestment. Then I engaged in meditation. My kerosene supply was low. I was using an Eskimo stone lamp filled with seal blubber. Frequently I had to interrupt my meditation to blow it up. Finally, when I thought everything was ready, I began Mass.

Ordinarily, before Mass on a winter morning, I took care to thaw out the sacramental wine. That morning my mind was flooded with memories brought on by the occasion, and I forgot to do so. Reaching the Offertory, I found myself searching under my bed for the bottle. The wine, of course, was frozen solid. The rest of the Mass had to wait until I could thaw out the wine by rolling the bottle between my hands. After Mass, I renewed my vows according to custom.

For breakfast, I cooked two slices of my last slab of bacon. I had long since consumed my last bread, so I baked some bannocks, flat griddle cakes made of oatmeal. Next came the dogs' breakfast. I hacked up a seal for them. They got double rations in honor of the feast day. The seal's head I kept. Later I fried the brains in grease left over from the bacon. They made a delicious lunch.

I was pulling at my pipe and washing the dishes when there was a clamor at the door. A panting Eskimo charged in. His little son, he said, had gashed his face.

"The way he's bleeding, Falla," he cried, "I'm sure he's dying, dying!"

I followed the man to his igloo. The boy had a deep cut in his forehead all right and it was bleeding profusely. His lusty bawling, however, assured me he would probably live to bury us all.

I had just finished sewing up the boy's wound when an Eskimo woman rushed into the igloo. My dogs, she informed me, had pulled out their line. They were having a battle royal among themselves.

A few minutes later, I was among the dogs, shovel in hand.

It didn't take long to stop the fight, and I came out with only one wound. To be exact, the wound was to my pants—a long, wide rip that had me flying to the mission house for needle and thread. By the time my pants were patched, it was time to read my breviary, then time for supper.

The smell of cooking brought a gang of Eskimos pushing into my narrow shack. I gave them a feast of tea and frozen fish. Well fed, they listened for an hour while I spoke to them of God. As usual, we rounded off the evening with storytelling and singing.

So things went during those early months in Victoria. Little by little, they improved. Today, at Sunday Mass, I face a sizable congregation. Even for the weekday Masses, there are almost always a few Eskimos on hand.

At Minto, Tom Goose brought me my first new parishioner. It all started one spring morning when word reached me that the wife of an Eskimo, whom Tom and I called Patsy, had just given birth to a baby.

"Boy or girl?" I asked.

"A girl," I was told.

I started out for Patsy's igloo at once. A terrible thought speeded my steps. I have already told you how frequently Eskimo parents kill their newborn girls. Lately, too, the hunting had been bad. Food was scarce. Under the circumstances, Patsy would not think twice about taking his new baby out to a quiet spot and stoning it to death. Unless—unless I could stop him!

As I approached the igloo, I saw Patsy coming out. Sure enough the baby was in his arms.

"Hey, there!" I called to him. "I hear you are a new father."

Patsy's greeting was an angry scowl. I disregarded it. I glanced at the baby, and then straight into Patsy's eyes. "Look here," I said, "were you by any chance thinking of doing away with this infant?"

Patsy shrugged. "And why not, Falla? After all, it is only a girl."

"Only a girl!" When I first came among the Inuit they gave me a nickname. *Il-a-ra-nai-tok*, they called me. It means "the one who is never angry." Well, the laugh was on them. I was angry at Patsy that morning! I was plenty angry, and I showed it. "Only a girl," I stormed. "You know better than to talk to me like that. You know my beliefs. Boy or girl—in God's eyes, they are equally precious!"

"But, Falla, there is so little food, and we have so many mouths to feed."

Just then a thought struck me—a good one, too. "Patsy," I said, "take that baby back into the igloo. Keep it warm and snug. I'm going away, but I'll be back in half an hour. When I return, I want to see the baby safe and sound."

Patsy was shaking his head.

"Do as I say," I ordered. Then, a little more softly, "Do it as a personal favor to me."

"Oh, very well, Falla. As a personal favor to you."

My next stop was in a little wooden shack Tom Goose had built for himself and his wife alongside the mission house. "Tom," I burst in, "how would you and your wife like to become the parents of a baby girl?"

"Oh, Falla!" Tom's face rebuked me. "You must not joke about such things. You know that we prayed for children and that the good Lord has not seen fit to answer our prayers."

"But I am not joking. Patsy has a new baby girl. He does not want her. Only just now I had to stop him from killing her. Suppose I ask him to give her to you?"

Tom and his wife hurried with me across the snow to Patsy's igloo. The baby, swaddled in furs, lay on the skin bed. Eskimos seldom show emotion, but when Tom's wife lifted the furs and saw the face of the little girl who might be hers, she burst into tears.

"So pretty," she said. "So very pretty."

Indeed, the little thing was unusually pretty.

Even when she knotted up her face and let out a long, loud squall, she was pretty.

"There you are, Patsy," I said. "Tom and his wife will take the baby off your hands."

I expected Patsy to hand the infant over then and there. I had misjudged my man. A sly, oily look crept over his face. "Falla," he said, "you are asking me to give up my own flesh and blood."

"Oh, come now!" I spoke with some amazement. "Only a few minutes ago you were going to kill the baby."

"Only a few minutes ago," he said, "things were different. Now Tom wants the baby. You cannot expect me to give my own child to another man without payment."

For a second I didn't know whether to laugh or cry. What I did was explode. "Patsy!" I thundered. "I thought I had met the world's greatest hypocrites, but you go to the head of the class." I turned to Tom. "Well?" I asked him. "What can you give him for the baby?"

Tom stole a look at his wife and dropped his eyes. "Nothing," he said sadly. "You know how it is at our house these days; we have nothing to give him."

"All right then," Patsy said, picking up the baby, "I will keep the dear little thing myself."

"You will do nothing of the sort." I took the

baby from him and shoved it into the arms of Tom's wife.

"But, Falla!" Patsy confronted me, trying hard to look like an outraged father. "Did you not hear Tom? He cannot pay anything for the baby."

"Don't worry. I'll see to that."

Early in the afternoon, with the happy parents standing by, I baptized the tiny girl, giving her the name of Elizabeth. Then I returned to Patsy's igloo to deliver his payment. I handed him a pair of pants, twenty pounds of flour, and ten pounds of sugar.

He received them chuckling. He was still chuckling when I left the igloo. Crawling through the entryway tunnel I could hear him yelling at his wife. "Did you see how I cheated the Falla?" he shouted gleefully. "A pair of pants and all this food for one useless girl!"

I could have told him, of course, that a soul is priceless. It would have made no impression. He would simply have chuckled some more and told his wife that "Falla is a stupid Big Eyebrows, a real ignoramus."

A few months after the baptizing of Tom's foster baby, a great event occurred. Even now I cannot think of it without feeling a warm glow around the heart. I received a chalice, a beautiful one. Engraved on it were these words:

PIUS XI, VICAR OF CHRIST, TO THE HERALDS OF CHRIST.

With the chalice was a white card reading, "From the Holy Father, with His Apostolic Benediction."

What was the story behind this? A few words will tell it. During the preceding year, my bishop had journeyed to the Vatican in Rome to report on his work. "Holy Father," he said during an audience with the Pope, "we are building on Victoria Island a mission to the last people on earth. We call it the Mission of Christ the King."

A smile lighted the Pope's features. "May our Lord reign up there," he said, "as He must everywhere. We ourself would like to contribute to your work."

The Pope used the expression "we ourself" because it is the custom of the Holy Father always to speak of himself as "we."

"For the Mission of Christ the King," he told my bishop, "we will give you a chalice after first saying Mass with it ourself. With this chalice the missionary priest on Victoria Island shall offer the Holy Sacrifice in our name for the extension of Christ's Kingship to the final frontiers of the world."

Shortly after I received the Pope's chalice,

I was visited by my good friend, Bishop Fallaise, the priest who had founded the first permanent missions to the Copper Eskimos. On a blowy winter evening in the little mission shack at Minto, the bishop baptized ten adult Eskimos and blessed three marriages. At midnight, he said a Pontifical Mass, gave First Communion to all and Confirmation.

For the Pontifical Mass, everything was missing *except* the bishop. There was no cape, no miter, no crosier. But Bishop Fallaise enjoyed every minute of it. To look at his happy face, you might have thought he was celebrating Mass at St. Patrick's in New York, or at St. Peter's in Rome.

After the Mass, he took my hand. "Father Buliard," he said, "I want to congratulate you on the censer. It is a work of art."

I had to laugh. I had made the censer out of an old meat can.

"And you know, Father Buliard," the bishop went on. "There was something familiar about the smell of your incense."

"Naturally, there was, Your Lordship," I told him. "The stuff we burned in the meat can was my best sugar. I simply colored it a little in honor of the occasion."

13. THE GREAT BIRD

During my first year on Victoria Island, I became famous as a dentist. It happened by accident.

One evening, a group of Eskimos, men and women, were sitting around the mission shack at Minto. They were telling stories and singing songs as usual.

Suddenly, the largest Eskimo in the crowd threw himself on the floor, writhing and howling at the top of his voice.

"*Sapristi!*" The French slang word burst from my lips as I hurried to him. "Whatever is the matter with you?"

His answer was a frightened look. Tom Goose had dropped to his knees beside me. "It's his tooth, Falla," he said.

"His tooth?"

"Yes, it's been hurting him for weeks."

"Let me see the tooth." I reached for the suffering hunter on the floor, but he squirmed away from me with another ear-splitting howl.

"Shut up," I yelled at him, "and let me have a look at that tooth." I had learned long since that the only way to get an Eskimo to behave is to treat him firmly. Often, in fact, it is a good idea to be a little rough.

I shook the big hunter into silence. "Now," I said, "open your mouth and point to the tooth."

He did so, whimpering all the time like an injured child. One look told me that the rotting molar was a goner. It would have to be removed fast.

I got a pair of flat pliers from my tool box and handed them to Tom. "Pull the tooth," I ordered.

"But what if it is stubborn, Falla?"

"Try it!"

Tom tried without success. Seizing the pliers from Tom, another Eskimo tried, also without success. After that, they all took turns. You would have thought it was some sort of game, the way they grunted and yanked, drowning out the patient's howls with their laughter. They all but took his head off, but the molar remained intact.

Finally, I grabbed the pliers, saying, "Perhaps I can do something."

On my first try, the tooth came out like a plucked flower.

After that, my services as a dentist were in great demand. As a doctor, too. My fame spread fast and wide. Soon I was pulling teeth and binding up broken limbs over all the island. Suffering Eskimos came hundreds of miles for treatment, or sent for me to go to them.

At midwinter I received a case far beyond my paltry abilities as a physician. The patient was a fifteen-year-old boy whom Tom and I had nicknamed Sailor because of his skill in manipulating the kayak, the Eskimo canoe.

Sailor was the son of Patsy, the same Patsy whose baby girl Tom and his wife had adopted. It was Patsy who brought the boy to the mission.

I boiled some water and handed a mug of tea to each of them.

"Falla," Patsy began in a sad voice, "I do not know what to make of this boy. Only last summer he was forever paddling out on the sea in his kayak. You remember, Falla? He caught more seals during the summer than you and I put together."

"I remember, Patsy," I said. "And now?"

"And now he only sits around the igloo. When he does move, he bumps into things. He is forever falling flat on his face."

"Forever falling?" I repeated, more to myself than to Patsy. I gave the boy a close look. Sitting on one of the mission house benches alongside his father, Sailor was the picture of health.

I racked my brain trying to think of some disease that would make a boy bump into things and fall down. Only one possibility occurred to me. Perhaps Sailor was suffering from epilepsy. I leaned forward, tapping the boy's knee with my hand.

"Sailor," I said, "do you hurt anywhere? I mean, do you get a pain in your head before you fall down?"

"Oh, no, Falla." Sailor shook his head vigorously. "There is no pain before I fall. Sometimes there is after."

"Where?"

"Wherever I hit myself."

I turned to his father. "Before the boy falls," I asked, "does he sometimes lose consciousness?"

"Oh, no, he falls with his eyes wide open. There is nothing unconscious about it. He simply bumps into something, stumbles, and cries bloody murder."

An idea had taken form in my mind. I had been reading my breviary when Patsy and his son came in. I held it up now, saying, "Tell me, Sailor, what color is this little book?"

Sailor leaned toward me, squinting his eyes. "Move closer," I suggested.

The boy took a few steps. "The book is black, Falla."

I hurried to the altar and lifted one of the candles. "And what color is this?" I asked.

Again he squinted, and again, "Come closer, Sailor," I told him.

There was a packing case on the floor. Sailor bumped into it. He would have fallen had not his father rushed over and grabbed him.

I went to the two of them. "You, Sailor, go next door and stay with Tom and his wife while I have a talk with your father."

When he was gone, I said, "Patsy, I'm afraid it's the boy's eyes."

"His eyes? You don't mean he is going blind?"

"I'm afraid so, Patsy."

"Do you have medicine for that, Falla?"

I shook my head.

Patsy came closer, his eyes full of hurt. "Then there is nothing you can do? Nothing at all?"

"There is something," I told him. "I can pray."

Patsy gave me a look of doubt. He was no Christian. He came often to the mission house and listened to my instructions, but it was my good tea and frozen fish that drew him, not my words.

After he had left, I sat for some time staring into space. For some weeks, I, myself, had been unwell. It was a toothache, sometimes violent, that came and went. Pulling out other people's teeth was one thing. My one attempt to pull my own had only made matters worse.

That evening, on my knees before my packing-case altar, I prayed long and hard. I said special prayers for two people, Sailor and myself.

A few weeks later, my prayers were answered. Toward evening, startled by the sudden barking of the dogs, I rushed outside just as a big sled came whizzing around the nearest hill. The sled driver was a young Eskimo with a round and grinning face.

"I come from the Hudson's Bay Company trading post, Falla," he shouted. "We have just heard a message for you on the radio. Your bishop has learned that you are not feeling well. He is sending an airplane to take you to Fort Smith to see the doctor."

I could have hugged him. "Come in! Come in!" I cried, flinging open the mission house door. Inside, I feasted him on my best bannocks and all that remained of my final slab of bacon. Then, summoning Tom, I sent him flying to fetch Patsy.

Tom was back in no time, an excited Patsy in tow. "Be of good cheer, Patsy," I shouted as they hurried in. "My bishop is sending someone to take me to Fort Smith. I will take Sailor along. There are many doctors in Fort Smith. They will make the boy's eyes well again."

Patsy's rough face became one big smile. "Oh, that is wonderful, Falla. Only . . . only . . . !"

"Only what, Patsy?"

"What is Fort Smith, Falla?"

I explained. Fort Smith is a huge village built by white men and filled with tall igloos.

"And where is it, this Fort Smith?"

"Far below the tree line, in a part of Canada known as the Northwest Territories."

The smile deserted Patsy's features. "But then, Falla," he moaned, "you cannot get to Fort Smith."

"Cannot get to it? Why not?"

"Because you cannot travel through the thick forests in a dog sled."

"But we will not go through the forests, we will fly over them."

"*Fly!*" Patsy's eyes opened so wide I thought they would fall out.

"Yes, Patsy, fly. We will go to Fort Smith in an airplane."

"An *airplane?*"

I glanced at Tom, at the young Eskimo from the trading post, at Tom's wife who had silently slipped into the cabin and was sitting on one of the benches. All three were laughing.

During my years at Coppermine the bishop had often visited us in his blue Waco airplane, but he had never come to Victoria Island by air. The natives of Victoria had never laid eyes on an airplane.

"Look here, Patsy." I took him by the shoulders and faced him toward the door. "I don't want to have to explain an airplane to you and then have to say the same thing to every other Eskimo all over again. Fetch everyone, and I'll describe the airplane to the lot of you, once and for all."

He was on his way fast. Every villager was with him when he returned. They trooped in noisily. They lost no time seating themselves on the mission house benches. Patsy had told them just enough to whet their curiosities.

Before starting my explanations, I got a piece of paper and pencil. I drew a picture. It was no work of art, but it did bear a resemblance to the bishop's Waco.

I held it up, turning so that all could see it.

"Now this," I said, "is an airplane. It has wings, see? That thing in front is a propeller. When the propeller turns fast enough, the airplane lifts off the ground."

"It is a flying dog sled!" somebody yelled.

"A great bird!" from somebody else.

"Yes," I said, "it is a great bird."

"Is it tame?" somebody inquired.

"Is there enough seal meat in all the world to feed it?" another wished to know.

Over and over, patiently, I explained that the "great bird" was not a real bird. It was a machine that could carry human beings many miles through the air at a terrific speed.

Eventually, there was a general nodding of heads. "We understand," several of them said. "We understand perfectly."

But as they scrambled to their feet and tramped into the night, chattering among themselves, I had a feeling that many of them were still highly puzzled.

14. FORT SMITH

For days, the Eskimos talked of nothing but the great bird. I had described the roar of the engines, telling them that they would hear the airplane before they saw it. Every time the sea ice shifted, sending a booming sound along the horizon, I had visitors. The Eskimos would crowd into the mission house, yelling at the tops of their voices.

"We just heard a big noise in the sky, Falla. The great bird must be arriving."

But no great bird came. A week passed, two weeks, three weeks. Little by little the Eskimos' excitement gave way to doubt. Going from igloo to igloo on my missionary duties, I could hear them muttering among themselves.

"Perhaps the Falla made it all up," they complained.

"Perhaps he is only teasing us!"

"Perhaps there is no great bird at all!"

But there was. On a late March morning I detected the unmistakable rumble of its engine high in the sky. A few minutes later, I was standing on the shore surrounded by a crowd of chattering Eskimos.

A terrible snowstorm was raging. We could hear the plane, but we could not see it. The sound passed close over our heads. It went away and came back, went away and came back again. Every day, for three weeks, I had lighted a fire on the shore in front of the mission, knowing that its smoke would help guide the aircraft in. In the tearing winds of the storm, however, a fire would be of no use. I could only stand there with the Eskimos, waiting, hoping . . . I was beginning to think the pilot would never feel his way down when, suddenly, as though a trap door had opened in the clouds, the plane came into view.

At the sight of it, the Eskimos fell silent. Apparently my description had not prepared them for anything so large. They remained where they were, stone silent, as I met the plane and ran ahead, guiding it toward shore.

It ground to a stop on the sea ice just below the mission house. Three men stepped out. The first was Bishop Fallaise. I hurried forward to receive his blessing, shouting, "Welcome once again to Minto, Your Lordship!"

He drew me to my feet, his handsome face wreathed in smiles. "Did you think we were never coming, Father Buliard?"

"I was beginning to wonder."

"We were delayed, but we will waste no time here. The minute the storm clears, we'll head south. Are you ready to travel?"

"*We* are ready."

"We?" The bishop shot me a quizzical look.

I told him then about Sailor, Patsy's son. "The boy," I explained, "seems to be losing his eyesight. I thought if we could take him to Fort Smith, perhaps the doctors there . . ."

"Of course, of course," the bishop broke in. "We'll take him. We'll squeeze him into the plane somehow."

He introduced me to the men with him—the pilot and a young priest. We had almost reached the mission house when a loud and confused shouting at our rear brought us to a halt. Turning back we saw that, at long last, the Eskimos had got up courage enough to approach the plane. They were swarming over it, feeling every strut and bolt. I could hear the voice of Patsy booming above the others.

"A strange bird, a very strange bird!" I could hear him yelling. "Would you believe it? It does not have so much as a single feather!"

As long as I live I shall never forget that trip to Fort Smith in the spring of 1939. I shall never forget the reactions of Patsy's fifteen-year-old son. Sailor's eyes were in bad shape all right, but he could still see many things; and, of course, almost everything he saw was new and strange to him.

As we winged south and crossed the tree line, Sailor pressed his face against the plane window agog with excitement.

"Falla!" he cried. "Look below. Such a crowd of people. Why, the earth is black with them!"

I looked. There was not a soul to be seen. Sailor had mistaken the dense forests of Canada for a crowd of people. He had never seen a tree before.

As we hurried across the landing field at Fort Smith, Sailor stopped suddenly and tugged wildly at my arm. "Your rifle, Falla!" he cried. "Get your rifle. Quickly! It would be a shame to miss that caribou with the hanging stomach."

It was not a caribou, of course. It was a cow, placidly grazing in a near-by pasture.

A few steps farther, Sailor was in a dither again. Only this time he did not want to shoot; he wanted to run. He had seen his first horse, and, as he put it, "I don't mind a good healthy dog, Falla, but that one is just a little too big."

At Fort Smith, we took him to the Roman Catholic hospital run by the Grey Nuns. It was a great moment the next day when the doctors made their report. Sailor's vision could be saved. A short series of treatments, and his eyes would be as good as new.

As soon as Sailor's treatments were finished, the two of us went on a sight-seeing tour. After years in the lonely north, I was delighted with the bustle of the little trading town. So was Sailor, and the sight of his laughing, happy face added greatly to my own pleasure. He could not gawk enough at the tall buildings, the parks, and the bright lights.

His first encounter with a stairway was one for the books. We were staying at Bishop Breynat's house. As we approached the stairway to the second floor, Sailor stood stock-still. At the hospital, he had traveled to and from his room in an elevator. He had never set foot on a stairway.

"Look here, Sailor," I said. "It's easy. You just lift your feet and climb, like this." I walked up a few steps to show him.

He followed, clinging to the banister with both hands and taking plenty of time.

I waited for him at the top of the stairs. "Now," I said as he joined me there, "suppose we walk down."

"Down!" He almost screamed.

"Sure. It's as easy as coming up. You just walk. See!" I started down the stairs. I had gone about half way when I heard a series of noisy thumps behind me. I turned in fright, certain that Sailor had lost his balance.

I need not have worried. A big grin on his face, Sailor was gaily sliding down the stairs. He had simply seated himself on the top step and shoved off. "Walking up is all right, Falla," he cried, "but I'll never walk down."

He never did. Although we spent many days in Fort Smith, Sailor always sat down to descend the stairs.

It was during the visit to Fort Smith that my superiors and I decided to set up the permanent mission on Victoria Island at King's Bay, its present site. Midsummer found me at Aklavik, a small Canadian city at the mouth of the Mackenzie River. There supplies and materials for erecting the new mission house were purchased and loaded aboard a Hudson's Bay Company schooner.

On August 16, I was at King's Bay, ready to work. I did not have to build the mission house alone. Helping me were a young Oblate brother and my old pal, Father Lucien Delelande, who, a few years before, had been my boss for a time at Coppermine. It was good to have tall and vigorous Father Lucien around. It was good to hear his hearty voice and to watch the smile that hardly ever left his lips.

The short Arctic summer was drawing to its close as we started building the combination chapel and living quarters of Christ the King Mission. The days were blustery. For shelter we had a little tent. It was much too small for three big men and far from watertight. The tent could have been higher, too. It was about right for a fellow my size, but when Father Lucien said Mass, he had to dig a little hole in the ground to stand upright.

We worked sixteen hours a day, Sundays included. By Christmas, the mission house was ready. In a way, I was sorry. Its completion meant I would lose my good companions, Father Lucien and the Oblate brother. There was work for them to do elsewhere. Shortly after New Year's Day, 1940, I carried them to Coppermine by dog team.

When I returned to my big new house at King's Bay, I was a little lonely at first. That passed, of course. For sixteen years, I lived in that house. I grew to love it. It was the center of my missionary work on Victoria Island.

It was in that house, during the long and lonely winters, that I began to write down the little I had learned about the Eskimos. I have shared some of this knowledge with you. Now I must tell you some other things. I must tell you how Inuk earns his daily bread, that is, how and for what he fishes and hunts.

15. "OUR DAILY BREAD"

Fish, of course, is one of the basic foods of the Inuit. They eat it any old way—raw, frozen, dried, cooked. It is fed to the dogs. In fact, in some camps it is the only food the dogs get, meat being reserved for humans.

In the old days, the Eskimos caught their fish with harpoons. Sooner or later, every spring, a joyous cry went up in the Eskimo village.

"The Ik-ra-luk has arrived!" someone shouted. "The Ikraluk has arrived." Ikraluk is the Inuit's name for the pink-fleshed spotted sea trout which my Eskimos always refer to as salmon and which they prefer above all other fish. In the spring, as the ice begins to break, thousands of salmon start swimming in from the sea, heading up the river toward the spawning grounds where they will lay their eggs.

The minute the salmon arrived in the old days, every member of the village rushed to the river, carrying a load of rocks in his arms. With the rocks the Inuit built an artificial shallow in the stream, a little lake easily closed behind the fish. When the trap filled with salmon, everyone leaped into the shallow water, splashing, yelling, striking out with his harpoon.

Sometimes, instead of building a stone trap, the Inuit simply rigged a weir across the river. The weir was a sort of fence made of driftwood and rocks. Openings were left in the weir, openings through which the salmon were forced to swim. At each opening a man waited, a three-pronged harpoon in his hands. As the salmon passed through, they were slaughtered by the hundreds.

Here on Victoria Island the Inuit still like to try their skill with the three-pronged harpoon; but only for fun. Most of their serious fishing these days is done with nets purchased at the white man's trading stores. The nets are spread either on the inland waters, or out in the sea itself. When there is no ice, the nets are anchored by rocks—either to a sand bar in the sea or to the banks of a river; or they are simply lowered over the gunwales of a boat and dragged along.

In winter, the net is lowered through holes in the ice. Using a long pole planted in the snow, a line is rigged so that the net can be raised each day through two holes, one at either end, simply by hauling on the rope. Of course the holes freeze solid overnight and have to be reopened each time Inuk sails out on his dog sled to check his nets.

Fishing on the sea ice has its moments of great fun. I still get a laugh when I recall one of my first trips out on Victoria Island. A dozen or more Eskimos were with me, and I lowered my net in accordance with their shouted instructions.

The net was down and anchored, and I was dreaming of all the silver salmon I would pull up the next morning when—bing, bang! A sudden blizzard came howling through the western gully, slashing everything before it like an enormous knife. The next thing I knew I was flat on my face, spinning across the glassy ice like a plate.

There was no point trying to grab hold of a hummock of snow. Nothing could remain stationary in the face of that shrieking, cutting gale. I was not alone, either. On all sides of me, the Eskimos were down and sailing shoreward. So were the dogs. The frightened beasts tried to dig in with their claws, but it was no use. They only piled up one on another and went spinning along, snarling and yelping and dragging their sleds behind them.

I banged into the shore, grabbed hold of a protruding rock and looked about me. All along the shore, the Eskimos were sailing in one at a time, like packages coming down a baggage chute. I expected at any moment to hear a round of Eskimo swearing; but there I was mistaken. Every one of my companions was laughing his head off. In a matter of minutes, we had built a snow windbreak and were sitting contentedly behind it.

"We will stay cozy here till it goes away," I heard someone yell. "After all, what else can we do?"

"*Pirtok!*" another cheerful voice shouted. "Nothing—one can do nothing about it!"

It is when you are out on the trail that fish really come in handy. No matter how heavily you load your sledge, you sometimes run out of provisions. And then? Well, then, if you are near the sea and there is a lake or river near by, you fish.

Out on the trail, one time, Tom Goose and I ran out of eats.

"Never mind, Falla," said Tom. "The sea is right at our elbow here."

In the semidarkness of a late winter afternoon, we hurried down to the shore. I expected Tom to start fishing at once. Instead, he wandered along the shore for some distance, his eyes fixed on the ground.

"Whatever are you looking for?" I asked him.

"A place where there are plenty of fish."

"How can you tell which are the best places?"

"That way, Falla!" Tom was pointing at a pile of square rocks lying on the shore. "When an Eskimo discovers a place where the fish are plentiful," he explained, "he sets up a pile of rocks on the shore. Then the next fellow who comes along will know exactly where to drop his line."

The ice was six feet thick. That didn't discourage Tom. With his axe, he dug a hole right through. When the water spurted up like a geyser, Tom took a piece of strap from under his parka and a copper hook. He baited the hook with seal blubber and began to fish. Up and down went his arm, keeping the bait in motion—"jigging" is the Eskimos' name for this action. Up and down, up and down. In less than an hour he had three trout, one of them weighing in the neighborhood of thirty pounds.

The trout froze the minute they hit the air. They froze as hard as steel. Before eating them, we had to dig a wider hole in the ice and hold them under water a few seconds to thaw them a little. Then we consumed them, and they were delicious!

After supper, we crawled into the little igloo we had hastily thrown up before going fishing. I fell asleep thinking of the words of Christ:

"Again, the kingdom of heaven is like a net cast into the sea and gathering in fish of every kind. When it was filled, they hauled it out."

16. NANUK, THE BEAR

Inuk may catch a thousand fish, but he will never brag about it. But let him kill one polar bear, and he will talk about it for days. For the big white polar bear, often weighing as much as 1,500 pounds, is the great prize in the eyes of the northern hunter.

Nanuk is the Eskimos' name for the big polar bear. The Inuit do not think much of Indians and white men, but they admire Nanuk.

"Nanuk," they say, "is almost as smart as

Inuk. He has twelve men's strength and eleven men's wit."

Nanuk is a mysterious fellow. At intervals he seems to disappear. For months no one will see a polar bear or even the tracks of one. Then one day, out of nowhere, Nanuk appears, waddling along in his stately, clumsy way, sometimes alone, sometimes with a comrade or two. Hunters have reported seeing as many as ten bears together.

The first time I spotted a polar bear, I was just plain shocked.

"What an enormous fat weasel!" I exclaimed.

That is about what Nanuk looks like. He has short legs, a long body, and an endless neck and slender snout. Lumbering along, he looks sleepy and cuddly and not in the least dangerous. Don't be deceived! In battle he is an all-out slugger. And when he wants to run away from you—or, worse yet, when he wants to run after you—he can gallop like a race horse.

Most of the time he simply trots, swaying from side to side because of his bulky rump. He can keep up a wobbly, steady trot all day, provided he hasn't had too much to eat. Food is his weakness. He loves to stuff himself. After doing so, he falls asleep, snoring like thunder, and so dead to the world you can walk right up to him without his awakening.

For the pleasure of gorging himself, Nanuk will take any kind of risk. He will walk right into a camp filled with dogs and men. He will even walk into a shack or igloo. He will filch seal right off a sled, although ordinarily he doesn't have to do this, being an excellent seal hunter himself. The blubber of seal is his favorite food. He doesn't care much for meat, except when times are hard.

He loves to play. Standing at a safe distance one day, I watched a big polar bear which had come across an empty steel oil drum. Nanuk was in ecstasy over his find. He rolled the drum down a hill; he pushed it back up. He did this a dozen times. Finally, tiring of the sport, he destroyed the drum and went lumbering away.

Another time I saw Nanuk playing with a dog sled someone had carelessly left in his path. He grabbed the sled gleefully and pulled it behind him. Coming to a steep hill, he simply hopped on and went sailing down, obviously having the time of his life.

His curiosity knows no bounds. Coming upon a boat lying upside down on the ice, he will sniff around furiously. Finally, determined to find out what is underneath, he will smash the boat with one swipe of his paw, splitting the hull as if it were cardboard. I lost two boats to Nanuk this way. Now I leave them keel down so that Mr. Nanuk can see there is nothing hidden. This works; with nothing out of sight to arouse his curiosity, Nanuk merely takes a short sniff and waddles on.

He is a smart hunter. In fact, the Eskimos observe him carefully. "We Eskimos," Tom Goose told me one day, "learned most of our hunting tricks from Nanuk. We watch how he does it, and then we do the same."

It was from Nanuk that the Eskimos learned how to hunt for Nathek, the seal, in the spring. It is something to watch Nanuk sneak up to a seal who has clambered up on a hunk of ice for a snooze. Advancing stealthily, Nanuk takes advantage of every shadow cast by the rough ice. When the ice is smooth, he moves very slowly, hiding his black snout by covering it with his white paw. Closer and closer he edges toward his prey, freezing like a statue every time Nathek, the seal, lifts his head to look around. Closer and closer. . . . Finally, getting close enough, Nanuk throws his huge body on the seal with unbelievable swiftness.

In winter, Nanuk goes confidently after seal living under six feet of ice. Again his methods are perfect. Locating the seal's breathing hole, he carefully thins out the ice around it so that when the seal comes up for air, he can grab him easily. Having thinned the ice, Nanuk covers it with snow so that the seal will not notice anything out of the way. Then Nanuk sits beside the hole, his left paw poised, ready to strike. He sits like this for hours, deadly still. He concentrates so hard that at this point you can walk right up to him and kill him on the spot.

"Of course," Tom Goose said to me one morning with a sly wink, "the smart thing is to wait until Nanuk grabs his seal. Then you get not only a fine bear, but a seal besides!"

Every mother bear teaches her cubs how to catch seal in the spring. I have seen a mother bear do this many times. She finds a breathing hole, thins out the ice, and then places her cubs around it. If one of them so much as moves a muscle, mama's big paw flashes out, and the little one receives a fierce spanking.

Once Nanuk has killed his seal, he settles down for a good meal. He tears the unfortunate animal apart. He gorges himself on the blubber, throwing the meat aside to be devoured later by his followers.

His followers? Yes. A group of little white foxes follow Nanuk almost everywhere he goes. They rely on the big bear to do their hunting for them. While he is eating, they try to snatch a bit from him. Nanuk will have none of this. He wants peace when he eats. It is comical to watch him shoo the little fellows away, warning them with his paw to wait until the boss is finished. When he has finally stuffed himself, he ambles off. Then the foxes gobble up whatever meat Nanuk has left behind.

Nanuk is a great traveler. You run into him everywhere. I have often come in from the trail to find a large polar bear snoozing on the mission house doorstep. Nanuk is sometimes found as much as 100 miles inland from sea, just wandering around, examining the scenery.

Of course he loves the sea. That's where the seals are—and the icebergs; nothing pleases Nanuk more than a joy ride on a swift, floating iceberg. He is a speedy swimmer, too, but in the water he is at a disadvantage when the hunters come. A bullet in the back of the head as he swims, and he is usually a goner.

One day, out sailing, I saw a churning wake of water ahead. "White whale!" I yelled to the boy at the helm. "After it!"

But it was no whale. It was a bear, swimming rapidly toward shore. As we made for him, he thrashed ahead fiercely, trying to outdistance us. We gained on him, and he turned his head in the water, showing his white teeth. Apparently aware that he could not outrun us, he whirled around suddenly and charged the boat. His idea was to strike it headlong and crush it, and he had more than enough strength to do it, too.

Twice he dived and came to the surface near the boat gunwales. Each time we managed to give him the slip. Finally, he surfaced in a great rage and swam straight toward the boat. I fired. The bullet struck a head bone, and Nanuk's head bones are hard. The bullet simply bounced off. It did leave a gash, the blood from which blinded the raging animal.

He floundered for a moment. Then he dived again, coming up right next to the boat, his jaws wide open. I fired again. This time, the bullet went home. The great white body floated away like a chunk of ice. We had only to fasten a line to him and tow him to shore—all thirteen feet of him. Then it was a matter of skinning and butchering and carrying the meat to the mission house.

This done, I did what any good Eskimo does after killing a bear. I stood on the front steps and shouted in a loud voice:

"*Na-nuk-to-rit-se!* Come and eat bear!"

I didn't have to yell long. Soon all the Eskimos in the vicinity were crowding into the mission house, and that night we had a great feast.

Nanuk is not ferocious. He rarely attacks a man unless he thinks he has good reason for doing so. He is quite intelligent. He often decides to run for it instead of putting up a fight. This is not because he is a coward; far from it. But sometimes, after looking the situation over, he decides to rely on speed instead of courage.

I remember one of Tom Goose's adventures with Nanuk. Tom went out to have a look at some traps he had set that day. The traps were near the Eskimo camp, so Tom did not bother to carry his rifle. Consequently, he felt a little nervous when, turning a bend in the trail, he found himself face to face with a good-sized polar bear.

To tell the truth, Tom assumed that his days on this earth were over. Nanuk bellowed, and Tom took to his heels. He really moved! When he finally stopped, out of breath, he was surprised to find himself still alive. He looked back, expecting to see Nanuk running toward him. But this was not the case. Nanuk was running all right—but in the opposite direction!

When Nanuk decides to fight, he does so with the fierceness of a regiment of marines. He simply will not give ground.

When she has cubs, Mrs. Nanuk is no one to trifle with, either. She will protect her young to the last breath. As soon as the sun is warm enough in the spring, the she-bear digs her way out of the snow house where she has hibernated for the winter and takes her offspring on their first outing. Her one thought is to protect them. eeing a hunter coming, she may bury the cubs ı the snow. Then she will lope off in another direction, hoping that the hunters will follow her and leave the cubs alone. More often, she will just stand and fight to the finish.

Cornered or wounded, an angry bear makes a large, but poor, target. He twists like a tornado. He has a trick of sliding toward you on his chest so that there is nothing to shoot at but his skull—and, as I've told you, his skull bones are hard and the bullet often glances off. Closing in, he rears up, for he kills, not with his teeth, but with his powerful paws. The hunter has a split second here. It was at this moment that the old-time Eskimo hunter, having no rifle, plunged his harpoon between the bear's shoulder blades or, pressing close against the beast, thrust to its heart with a knife.

An old Eskimo hunter one day gave me a bit of advice. "Falla," he said, "if you want to live to be as old as I am, shoot at a bear the minute you see him. Don't aim for the heart, either. Aim for his shoulder. That's what stops him every time."

I have followed his advice. As a result, I've brought down a good many bears, although there were times when Nanuk nearly brought me down instead.

When Nanuk falls, the Eskimo hunter approaches him cautiously. Perhaps Nanuk is dead. Perhaps not. He may be just pretending, trying to draw the man within range of his powerful paws.

Once the hunter is certain Nanuk is dead, he stands for a moment just looking at the huge beast. At this moment there is always a look of respect in the Eskimo's eyes.

"What a good fellow Nanuk is," he mutters to himself. "What a smart beast. Why, he is almost as smart at Inuk!"

17. NATHEK, THE SEAL

Tom Goose and I had been out on the sea ice all morning, hunting for Nathek, the seal. We traveled slowly, walking alongside our dog teams. It was early spring. Farther out, large cracks in the ice were blue with open water, but, on the whole, the snow-covered ice was firm under our feet.

It was a bright day. The great white Sahara around us sparkled under a fierce sun. We squinted our eyes as we moved along, looking hopefully about.

"This is not our lucky day, Falla," Tom grunted. "We have been out many hours, and still not a seal in sight."

"Be of good cheer, Tom. Our luck will change. In fact . . . !" I halted my dogs with a low-voiced order. "In fact," I repeated happily, "it *has* changed."

Tom shielded his eyes with a hand as he followed the direction of my gaze. Stretched out alongside a crack of open water, less than 200 yards away, was a magnificent specimen of the squareflipper, the big bearded seal.

Tom peered and grunted. "And do you think, Falla," he asked, "that you can get that one?"

"Of course I can get him."

"Want to bet?"

"You know very well that I'm not a betting man, Tom."

"Very well." Tom chuckled. "I will only say then that I do not think that you can kill that squareflipper."

"And I will say that I can!"

I was already down on the ice, crawling along, crawfishing this way and that, making like a seal.

For some twenty-five yards I squirmed across

the ice, splashing through pools of water. Every second I expected the napping squareflipper to lift his head and look about him the way seals do. I squirmed another ten yards, and another ten. Still no movement on the part of the seal.

"How odd," I thought. "It isn't like Nathek to sleep so long without looking around." Another few yards and I would be close enough to get a good shot at him. "Oh, well," I thought, covering the remaining distance with a quick crawl, "if that old squareflipper hasn't sense enough to protect himself . . ."

I was near enough. Leaping to my feet, I fired. Echoing back to me came the harsh thud of a bullet hitting bone. Obviously I had got him square in the head. Even so, I ran to him fast. A squareflipper is tough. My bullet might have simply stunned him, in which case he would be off that ice and into the water fast when he recovered.

I threw myself on the big black mammal. One feel of his hairy hide and I understood why Tom had said I would never kill that seal.

He was already dead! He had been for hours!

I could hear Tom coming up behind me. He was sputtering with laughter. "How about it, Falla?" he shouted. "Aren't you glad you didn't bet me any money?"

"*Sapristi!*" I turned to him. "Please tell me,

Tom. How did you know this seal was already dead?"

"By the way he looks."

"Looks?"

"Yes. Observe this seal closely. He has a flat look. A live seal has a round look. That's how you tell the difference."

"I'll remember that," I told him.

"Don't bother, Falla. At a distance no Big Eyebrows can tell the difference between a dead seal and a live one. Only Inuk can do that."

A few days later, Tom and I were out hunting seal again.

We parted company for a short time, and, during Tom's absence, I happened to drop my rifle into a crack of open water. Sounding for it I brought up not only the gun, but a long-dead seal.

At that moment I heard Tom's voice in the distance, and a wild idea hit me. Quickly I laid the dead seal on the ice, curling it into the position Nathek takes when he cat naps. Then, hurrying across the ice, I hid myself behind a high hummock of snow.

Soon Tom appeared. Of course he saw the seal lying there. And of course he did just as I had hoped he would. Flinging himself down, he hastily crawled to within shooting distance of what he thought was a sleeping seal. Hastily he fired, hitting his target, Nathek's head, squarely, and flung himself on the seal.

Just as hastily he jumped to his feet, uttering an exclamation of disgust!

I had reached his side by this time, and was I tickled! For the first time since coming to Eskimoland, I had the satisfaction of seeing an Eskimo laugh at himself.

"So," I yelled at him, "you Inuit can always tell a dead seal from a live one."

"Oh, well, Falla. You know how we are. Sometimes we—well, we brag a little." And Tom broke into a roar of laughter.

The Inuit, of course, hunt for seal all the time, in all seasons. In winter, they catch Nathek at his breathing hole, as I've already told you. In summer, they go to sea in their kayaks, their white skin canoes. When you are hunting swimming seals in summer, the important thing is to hit them in the head. With a bullet in his body, the seal tends to sink at once. If you hit him in the head, he usually will float long enough for you to pull him in with your harpoon.

It is great sport hunting Nathek in open water. For the Inuit, to be sure, it is more than a sport. It is a necessity. The seal is their only source of fuel, and, without fuel, life would be impossible in the great white desert of the north.

18. CARIBOU HUNT

Late one winter Tom and I made a missionary journey to some inland camps. On our third day out, we drove our dog teams up a high mountain, running with them all the way. The snow was soft, making the going difficult. Reaching the top, I was about to throw myself down when Tom suddenly seized my arm.

He was more excited than I had ever seen

him. "Below, Falla!" he shouted. "Look below! *Tuktuk!*"

Tuktuk is the Inuit's name for the caribou, the shaggy North American reindeer.

I looked down. In the sweeping white scoop of the valley was an enormous herd of caribou. Thousands of them, they milled slowly forward under a forest of swaying antlers.

I turned to Tom, and my wide-mouthed look of amazement amused him.

"Is that not a sight!" he cried. "Do you know what you are looking at, Falla?"

"Of course I know. Caribou!"

"But that is not just any old caribou. You're looking at the main herd."

The main herd? Rarely, as I've told you, do you see a caribou by himself. Ordinarily he travels in a herd. There are many small herds, and there is one fabulously large army of caribou known as the main herd of the Barren Land.

In their igloos, at night, the Inuit tell many stories about the great herd. They relate how the main herd roams endlessly over the steppes, endlessly seeking an area where moss and lichen grow plentifully under the snow. Every Eskimo claims to have seen the main herd at least once. Actually, many live and die in the Barren Land without ever laying eyes on it. And now Tom and I, standing on the peak of a snow-carpeted mountain, were looking at it! We shuddered at the sight as, descending, we plunged into the midst of the animals.

Our trail lay straight through the herd. The big, gentle animals went right on grazing. Only once in a while did a huge bull toss his antlers skyward and give us a mildly quizzical look. Frightened by the sheer bulk of the herd, our dogs pulled steadily ahead, making no effort to go after the slowly moving caribou.

Occasionally a score or so of caribou would leave the herd. Loping away together, they would graze for a while in some distant area. Whenever this happened, the caribou of the main herd waited and halted. Not until the smaller group rejoined the herd did they lumber onward into the wind.

Along the outer edges of the herd trotted small packs of gray, long-haired wolves. Mean-looking fellows they were, with their greedy eyes and sharp snouts. The wolves did not dare attack the herd. But, as we were going down the mountain in the morning, Tom and I saw a single caribou stray away by himself; then there was a massacre.

The wolves chased him cross country. Catching up with him they attacked in a body, slashing at his neck and hacking at his feet with their terrible teeth. One, then two, then three of the wolves leaped on his back and rode him. Even before the caribou was dead, they were tearing huge strips of meat from his body.

It took us two days to make our way through the undulating sea of animals—two days that I shall never forget!

When the members of an Eskimo camp hear that a caribou herd is near by, they organize a community hunt. They ambush the caribou between two hills, or two lakes, or in some decline through which the caribou must pass.

Waiting for the caribou to arrive, they hide behind rocks, rifles ready. The lead group of the herd is allowed to pass through. Once the lead group goes through, the other caribou come along behind it like sheep. Then the Inuit fire, and in a few minutes the plain is covered with hundreds of dead and dying caribou. The surviving members of the herd, frightened and bewildered, charge on, heedless of the fallen.

It is a sad thing to witness, the slaughter of so many caribou at once. But what can the Inuit do? As Tom Goose said one day, "We live in a hard and cruel country. Somehow we must feed and clothe ourselves. And to feed and clothe ourselves, we must kill caribou in great numbers."

19. SPORT AND DRAGON

Inuk, as I've told you, thinks highly of Nanuk, the bear. "Nanuk," he says, "is almost as smart as Inuk."

This is nothing compared with what he says about the dogs who pull his sledge in winter and pack his belongings in summer.

"What do I think of my Huskies?" an old Eskimo said one day in answer to a question from me. "Why, they are too wonderful to describe. I would sooner lose my wife and children than one of my dogs. My dogs are as good as me. The only difference between them and me is that they cannot speak; that's all!"

The Huskies are, indeed, wonderful dogs. They are world-famous for their magnificent build and smart pace. It is an inspiring sight to behold a well-matched team of Huskies, their bushy tails proudly rolled up their backs, straining at the sled anchor, raring to go.

The Husky dog is short and stubby. His body is round and compact. He may weigh only seventy pounds, or as much as a hundred, but every ounce is bone and muscle and tough as leather. He can pull his weight and more all day long, for days at a time. In winter, the thick wool which blankets his body, between his real hair, enables him to withstand cold. He travels unconcernedly in the worst snowstorm. At night, rolling himself into a ball, he sleeps happily in the snow.

Once, on a night of extremely bitter cold, I built a shelter for my oldest dog and led him to it. He sniffed at it and looked at me. Then he walked around to the windy side of the shelter and curled up. Just before he went to sleep, I could have sworn that he gave me a wink, as if to say:

"It's very nice, your shelter, old man, and I thank you. But, you see, I like to be able to smell into the wind. Just in case someone should come along, you know!"

Among themselves, the Huskies fight often and viciously. Favor one member of your team, and you sign his death warrant. Coming out some morning to check the line to which the dogs are tied for the night, you will find your favorite dead. The others, jealous of the extra attentions he has received, have done him in.

None of this ferociousness appears in their treatment of you, their master. To you, the Eskimo dog is all gentleness, all love, all loyalty.

In the spring, the Arctic sea ice is needle sharp. Every step a Husky takes leaves paw marks in blood. Behind your sled, the trail is marked by two bright red lines. Despite the pain, the dogs pull their hearts out. After all, you are driving the sledge and you are the master. For you, they will gladly die in their tracks.

Sometimes two of them become friends—for example, Sport and Dragon of my own nine-dog team.

Sport and Dragon were huge dogs. They had the same build and the same coloring, white with black heads. They became such fast friends that they even shared their food, something an Eskimo dog hardly ever does.

Dragon was the quiet one, all kindness. He

was aware of his enormous strength, but he was never eager for a fight.

Sport was the peppery type with a chip on his shoulder. He regarded himself as Dragon's defender. At the first snarl at Dragon from another dog, Sport would charge, his lip curling, his teeth showing. Sometimes Dragon was just an excuse. Sport liked to fight. He liked to take on every new dog and give him a licking just to show who was boss.

In such fights, he always used the same methods. The first bound carried him clear of the dogs surrounding the new dog. The second took him to the newcomer's throat. Then he would shake the new dog, dragging him about in the snow. Finally, he would pin him to the ground like a wrestler.

I always got there too late. Sport, having thrashed the other dog silly, would look at me with what was almost a smile of satisfaction. Half the time I hadn't the heart to give him the thrashing he deserved. Back at Dragon's side, he would wink at his pal.

"See?" he seemed to be saying to Dragon. "He's a softy, that Father Buliard. Just a softy!"

To part Sport and Dragon when you harnessed up was to invite trouble for Sport's new teammate. Occasionally I did part them in order to team Sport with some lazy dog who needed a little waking up. Whenever I did this, Sport made life miserable for the other dog until I put him back with his friend Dragon. Then it was touching to watch the way the two pals encouraged one another, rubbing noses over the ropes as they trotted along.

Yes, Sport and Dragon were inseparable until—until, swimming a river one summer day under a heavy pack, Dragon went to the bottom and drowned!

Tom Goose and I still talk about that day. We talk about how Sport, seeing his pal go under, raced back and forth along the shore, crying like a child. In the end, Tom and I had to take him away from the place by force.

Back at the mission house, we tied him up. He howled day and night. Every bark from one of the other dogs brought his head up sharp. You could tell from the miserable look in his big eyes what he was thinking.

"Could that be my pal Dragon?" he was asking himself.

Of course it wasn't. Dragon was gone forever, and, in time, Sport seemed to realize it. He refused to eat, quickly turning from a powerful Husky into a sack of bones. There was no point in harnessing him to the sled; he simply refused to move. Tom and I tried everything we could think of to revive his spirits. We fed him special tidbits and gave him extra attention. Nothing worked. Sport wanted nothing—nothing but Dragon.

I was about to shoot him to shorten his misery when Tom came up with an idea.

"Look here, Falla," he said, "you know that little pup in the mission house, the one called O-mik-mak?"

"Yes, I know the one called Omikmak. What about him?"

"He's Dragon's son. Bring him out, Falla. Put him near Sport. After all, the puppy has Dragon's smell. Perhaps Sport will take to him."

I hesitated a moment. "Perhaps Sport will take to the pup," I said, "and then again, perhaps he will simply lift a paw and kill him."

"Do you want to save Sport or not, Falla?"

"You know I do."

"Then, we'll have to take the risk."

In the mission house I picked up little Omikmak, Dragon's son. He was a tiny pup, a ball of fur scarcely larger than my hand. Bringing him outside, I sat him down alongside Sport. Then Tom and I stood back and waited—and hoped!

At first Sport did not even look at the little fellow beside him. He remained seated on his haunches, his mournful eyes staring into space.

Then, slowly, very slowly, he turned his head. The puppy was edging away, frightened and whimpering, when Sport jumped at him.

I jumped myself. "That's the end of little Omikmak!" I mourned.

But Sport did not kill the puppy. For some time he simply kept him on the ground under his paw. He looked him over, sniffing carefully.

His eyes told him that this little thing couldn't possibly be his old friend Dragon. But his nose told him that it was! Suddenly a quiver ran through his big body, and he broke into a frenzy of delighted barks!

Tom and I grabbed each other's hands and danced!

Sport was saved! He made a pal of little Omikmak in the same way he had made a pal of his father, Dragon. He began to eat again. Soon he was back on the team, pulling with the other dogs. Soon he was fighting all comers, always ready to defend Omikmak, just as he had defended his father before him.

Sport lived to be very old. When he could no longer pull with the team, I sent him down to Burnside, Canada, to live at the mission conducted there by my friend, Father Lucien Delelande. Unable to work, Sport became the mission house watchdog, a job he took very seriously to the end of his days.

Coming home from a long missionary journey one morning, Father Lucien found the grand old dog dead on the doorstep. I like to think that Dragon came for Sport during the night and that somewhere, in some sort of Arctic dog heaven, they are having a rollicking time together.

Perhaps you think I am making too much fuss over mere dogs. Well, to us "poor parsons of the North," the dogs who pull our sleds are mighty important. They are our faithful servants and our good companions. They live and die in a great cause. As the Eskimos say, "They are as good as we. The only difference is that they cannot speak. That's all!"

20. THE POOR PARSONS OF THE NORTH

"All you need to be a missionary to the Eskimos," my bishop once told me, "is a strong back and a good guardian angel."

The back cannot be too strong. To transport supplies to the missions, the bishop years ago purchased a ship known as the mission schooner and called it *Our Lady of Lourdes*. Many times I have seen the bishop himself unloading a cargo of coal from *Our Lady*, his face streaked with black and a happy tune on his lips.

At Stanton, a mission on the Arctic Ocean some 600 miles west of Coppermine, the priests become woodsmen every spring. Journeying south below the tree line, they spend many days cutting logs for their winter fuel. At another mission, there is a coal mine. There the fathers disappear underground for weeks. With picks and dynamite, they take out their winter fuel supply.

The Arctic missionary must be a jack-of-all-trades: traveler, hunter, fisherman, igloo-builder, sledge-maker, boatbuilder, carpenter, cabinet-maker, tinsmith, electrician, engine mechanic, radio man, dentist, and surgeon. The corner drugstore is a long way off. The nearest is 2,000 miles away. The nearest regular doctor is not much closer. My friend, Father Lucien, a great amateur physician, once remarked:

"Well, none of my patients has died yet. If one did, he'd be pretty lucky, having me right there beside him, ready to administer the last sacraments!"

As I come to the end of this story, I have only one regret. I wish there were space enough to tell you the stories of all my friends among the hard-working Catholic missionaries of Eskimoland. Let me, just as an example, mention one.

His name is Father Franche. He came north

as my helper in 1936 and spent some months with me at Coppermine. Father Franche loves an engine of any kind. Complain of a spark plug, and a few minutes later your outboard motor will be spread all over the Northwest Territories while Father Franche carelessly tosses the parts about. Don't be alarmed. Soon he will have your engine singing like a bird, and as good as new again.

Father Franche's pipe is part of his face. He is never without it. At Aklavik, Canada, one time, he shocked the sisters and amused the congregation when he entered the chapel very dignified indeed. But the dignity took a beating when the surplice he was putting on got hooked in that pipe, which was in its usual place—between his teeth.

For a number of years Father Franche has been the skipper of the mission schooner *Our Lady of Lourdes*. I have sailed as a member of his crew many times. Again and again I have seen him face the worst of Arctic storms with what Mark Twain called "the confidence of a Christian with four aces." A great pioneer is Father Franche, a great priest.

But then, so are they all, my comrades, my Oblate brothers, "the poor parsons of the North."

"Falla," Tom said to me as we set out on

the trail one windy and snowy morning, "sometimes I wonder about you missionaries."

"What do you wonder, Tom?" I asked.

"Why you do it. You travel 500 miles just to help one sick Eskimo, and then another 500 just to baptize a couple more. You work so hard and get so little out of it. Sometimes I think you missionaries are fools."

Right, Tom. We are fools. Fools for Christ, we are, and proud of it.

"Go into the whole world," He said, "and preach the gospel to every creature!"

Those are our marching orders, Tom, and march we must.